Atlas of Plant Life

Illustrated by
David Nockels & **Henry Barnett**
Consultant Anthony Huxley

Maps by Geographical Projects London

Herbert Edlin

Atlas of Plant Life

The John Day Company New York

Geographical Director **Shirley Carpenter**
Editor **Geoffrey Rogers**
Art Director **Frank Fry**
Design **Nigel Talbot**

The John Day Company, 257 Park Avenue South, New York, N.Y. 10010

An **Intext** Publisher

Published in Canada by Longman Canada Limited

Library of Congress Cataloging in Publication Data

Edlin, Herbert Leeson
    Atlas of plant life
        1. Botany—Popular works   2 Phytogeography
3. Plants, Cultivated   4. Vegetation and climate
I. Title
QK50.E3 1973   581   73-4361
ISBN 0-381-98245-9

Printed and bound in Spain by Novograph, S.L., Madrid

Contents

Introduction

ATLAS OF PLANT LIFE presents a continent-by-continent
review of the world's wild and cultivated plants. Full-colour
illustrations accompany the text and easily identifiable symbols
show distribution on attractive colour relief maps. Many of the
plants are shown in their natural settings, a presentation that
establishes the "atmosphere" of each region—from the dark,
impenetrable rain forest of central Africa to the brilliant flame
trees of south-east Australia. Crop plants are discussed in the
chapters covering their native homes and not necessarily in the
chapters featuring the areas in which they are now mainly
cultivated.

The text relates plant distribution to climate and other
natural factors and also to man's intervention—a theme that
is further explored in the final chapter, which looks at some
important examples of man-made plant migrations.

The plants described in ATLAS OF PLANT LIFE are
identified by their common names. In some cases the scientific
name has been added where confusion could arise with another
plant. Symbol keys accompanying the distribution maps are
arranged in alphabetical order of common names. A table on
page 124 lists the scientific names of the principal plants
described in the book.

1 Climate and Plants

The opening picture shows the wide range of plant life that flourishes during summertime in a northern European country with a temperate climate. Both warmth and moisture are, at this season, adequate for growth, yet every plant makes provision, in its life pattern, to endure the cold winter that will surely follow.

The simplest plan is that of the crimson clover, an annual plant, or plant of one year's duration, that has an active life-span of only six months. (The crimson clover is an exception among clovers, most of which last for several years.) In spring it sprouted from a seed, sent down a shallow root, and raised the shoot bearing the leaves that help to nourish it. Now it has opened its clusters of red blossoms, to attract the bees that will pollinate them. After fertilization, each flower in turn bends downwards and starts to ripen its seed-pod. Later the whole clover plant, including the roots, will wither and only the tiny seeds, lying dormant on the frozen winter soil, will remain alive to renew growth next spring.

Beside the clover grows the cocksfoot grass, so-called because its pale-mauve flower-spike resembles the spreading toes of a cock's foot. It is also known as orchard grass. This is a hardy perennial plant that, in contrast to the crimson clover, has a life-span of many years. Yet it, too, can only grow actively during the spring, summer, and early autumn. When the cold winter draws near, it transfers its food reserves from its leaves and stems to a thick rootstock below ground level, and all its foliage then fades and dies. Next spring, when warmth returns, it sends up fresh leaves from this rootstock. Around midsummer it opens its wind-pollinated flowers, which soon ripen fine seeds that are scattered on the winds. Some sprout on bare soil in autumn, but others lie dormant until the next spring, so giving the cocksfoot grass a second way of surviving the winter.

This same life pattern is followed by the tall reeds that

Oak (left) and hawthorns (on bank) are broad-leaved trees that shed leaves each autumn. Wheat (far field) and crimson clover (right foreground) pass the winter as seeds. Water lilies, waterside reeds and reed-maces, and cocksfoot grass (bottom right), die down to rootstocks in winter. Ivy and mistletoe (both on oak) remain evergreen.

flourish along the waterside, rooted in the mud just off the shore. But this perennial grass is adapted to grow in soil that is always waterlogged. It can win the oxygen it needs for its root growth from the water, which the cocksfoot grass cannot do. In winter, when all the tall reed stems are hollow, dull brown stalks, the stream may freeze over, but in its dormant state the reed survives safely, even below thick ice. The abundant seeds, which may be spread by wind, water, or both, also enable the reed to survive the cold season.

The white water lily that floats its blossoms and heart-shaped leaves on the water's surface is even more fully adapted to an aquatic life. A perennial, it spends the winter as a fleshy rootstock in the mud at the bottom of a lake or slow stream. There it can survive the cold, even when the water is ice-bound. When the spring warmth raises the temperature of the water, the lily sends up thick yet weak leaf-stalks. The water supports them as they grow, so they need little structural tissue. The broad flat leaves spread out on the water surface, and use the sun's direct rays for energy to absorb carbon nutrients from the air. The lily flower is easily found by the insects that carry pollen from one blossom to another. The large seeds ripen in a round pod above the water, fall into it, and eventually sprout next spring on a mud bank, possibly far downstream.

On the firm dry land the hawthorn bush provides a good example of a woody perennial plant that lives for many years, growing taller each year instead of dying back to ground level. It is seen here in its green leafy state, with bright white blossoms, open to attract pollinating insects. As autumn comes on, the leaves of the hawthorn, in common with those of other deciduous trees and bushes, will turn brown and fall, leaving bare stems standing through the winter months. Though the woody stems never die back, the hawthorn cannot keep its leaves active in the cold season, as they would lose more water than its roots could supply from the frost-bound soil, and the bush would die of drought. Next spring a fresh crop of leaves will open, while young green shoots will extend the branches' spread, becoming thicker as layers of woody tissue are formed within them. Hawthorn seedlings also spring up from the seeds that birds scattered as they devoured the autumn berries. This provides another way for the tree to survive the winter.

The tall oak follows the same rhythm of growth. Every autumn it loses its leaves, and every spring it puts forth fresh ones, extending its shoots at the same time. Its flowers consist of green catkins, which hold either all-male or all-female flowers. Oak pollen is spread by the wind. The oak's seed, the familiar acorn, ripens in autumn and passes the winter on the forest floor before sprouting the following spring.

The oak seedling takes many years to grow tall enough and large enough to bear flowers and acorns itself. Its stem must grow stouter as well as taller to carry the increasing weight of foliage and branches. This is achieved by a hidden layer of growth cells below the bark, called the cambium. Active, like the rest of the tree, only in spring and summer, the cambium lays down, each year, a fresh annual ring of timber on the

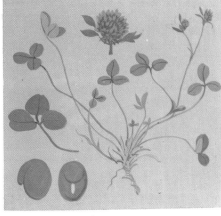

Crimson clover, an annual that sprouts from seeds (bottom left) in spring, flowers, forms seeds in pods, then dies in autumn.

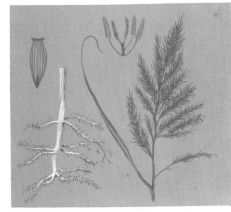

Common reed springs from perennial rootstocks in damp mud, flowers and develops seeds (top left) to aid its spread.

Hawthorn renews growth from buds on woody twigs each spring. White flowers develop red berries, holding seeds that birds scatter.

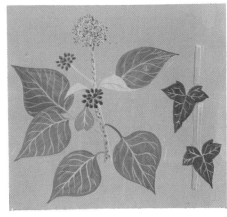

Long-lived, evergreen ivy climbs oak trunks, first bearing lobed leaves (right). When mature, it opens oval leaves (left), bears flowers, then berries.

Cocksfoot grass, a perennial, passes through winter as an underground rootstock. Left: flower spike, seed. Right: single flower.

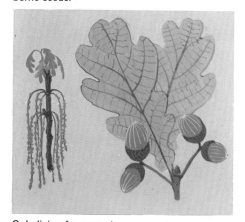

White water lily springs from fleshy stems rooted in pond bottoms (right). Flowers on the surface ripen water-borne seeds.

Oak, living for centuries, renews leaves annually. Left: male catkins. Right: acorns that ensure tree's spread.

Mistletoe forms a parasitic, evergreen bush rooted on oak stems. Birds carry sticky white berries to other trees, where seeds sprout.

outside of the pre-existing wood. In this way the oak's stem records the passage of the seasons that rule the life of every green plant in this northern country of forest and meadow.

Two plants shown in the picture break the general pattern of complete rest through winter's cold. One is ivy, a climber that often uses oak trunks for support, though it gets all its nourishment from the soil and the air. The other is mistletoe, which grows as a parasite on oak, and also on several other trees. It extracts its supplies of water and mineral salts from the host tree but uses its own green leaves to draw carbon compounds from the air. Both these plants bear thick leaves with waxy coatings that check water-loss, which explains why they stay green out of water when gathered for Christmas decoration. Holly, which often grows in the shade of oaks, has this drought-resistant property too. While the larger trees stand leafless in winter, holly and other evergreen plants (i.e. those that retain their leaves in winter) get ample sunlight; but during the summer months they are overshaded and so receive less light energy for active growth. (The plants described in this opening section are plotted on the maps in Chapter 2.)

We have seen how different plants develop life-forms and patterns of growth, to ensure that their basic needs are always met. These needs are simple, and are the same for most living plants. The accompanying picture of a petunia, an annual plant that grows from seed, shows how each part of a green plant fulfils its purpose.

Looking first below ground level, the plant's roots anchor it firmly in the soil, and take in the water that is essential for growth and every process of the plant's life. The free supply of water is checked, in most climates, either by dry seasons in which the soil holds too little water, or by cold seasons during which water is frozen into ice and cannot be carried up through the plant's tissues. In most regions, therefore, we find plants adapted to endure long interruptions of water supply.

Dissolved in the soil water, in minute amounts, are the mineral salts that are also necessary for the plant's life processes. Relatively large amounts of three elements, namely nitrogen, potassium, and phosphorus, are needed; a dozen others, including iron, magnesium, and calcium, must be present also, though only in small amounts. The character of the underlying rocks and of the soil affects their availability, but there are usually enough mineral nutrients for plant life, always provided that water is available to dissolve and transport them.

Water and mineral salts rise through the conductive tissues within the stem, to the leaves. Each leaf is a chemical factory in which the gas called carbon dioxide, present in minute quantities in the air, averaging only 3 parts of 10,000, is combined with water from the soil to form sugar. This process, called photosynthesis, is carried out in living green leaves with the aid of a complex chemical called chlorophyll. (Some plants, such as the copper beech, have leaves that contain chlorophyll and carry out photosynthesis but the green colour is masked by other pigments.) The energy needed comes from sunlight.

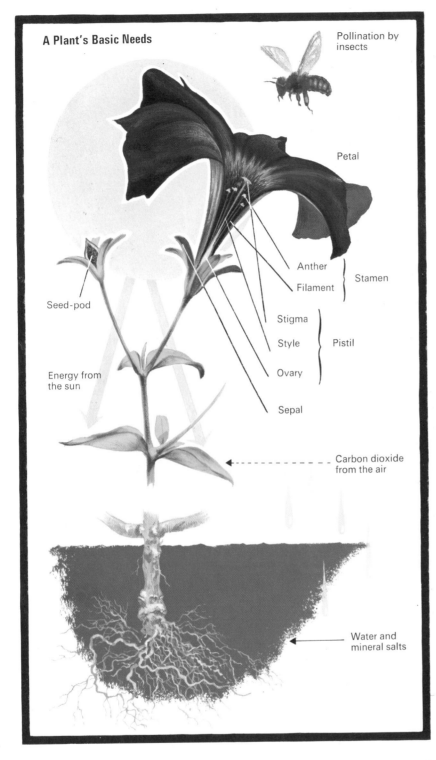

A Plant's Basic Needs

Pollination by insects

Petal

Anther

Stamen

Filament

Stigma

Style — Pistil

Ovary

Sepal

Seed-pod

Energy from the sun

Carbon dioxide from the air

Water and mineral salts

Summer warmth enables the monkshood to spring vigorously from fleshy roots, in which food is stored through the winter.

Rock rose in Portugal bears leathery evergreen leaves that resist summer drought and continue photosynthesis through cool, rainy winters.

Like most plants, this petunia is anchored in the soil by the roots, which absorb water and mineral salts for the plant's basic processes. To make food by photosynthesis, the plant also needs sunlight energy and carbon-dioxide gas from the air. Oxygen gas is absorbed by the plant for the release of energy from food for growth processes. Warmth must be adequate for growth to occur. Insects bring fertilizing pollen from other petunia plants.

All green plants must therefore have daylight for their growth and in regions where the length of day varies, from summer to winter, they grow faster during the longer summer days.

The sugar formed in the leaf is carried, in its dissolved state, to all parts of the plant, including the roots. Most of it is changed, by chemical means and in association with other elements, into plant tissues. A small amount of the sugar is used by the plant, through combination with oxygen from the air, to provide energy for these growth processes. The growing points of the shoot, leaf, and flower buds, and the root tips, are particularly active in this way.

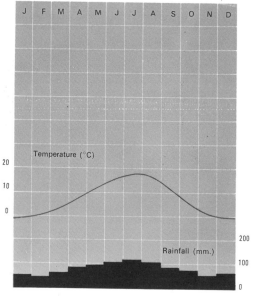

Zurich

In the monkshood's Swiss home moisture is always ample. But the temperature curve only exceeds 5° C from April to October.

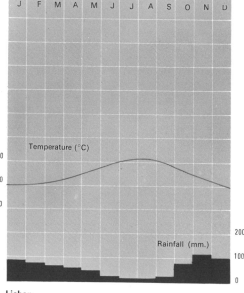

Lisbon

In Portugal, by contrast, temperature is always adequate for plant growth. But rainfall is insufficient from May to September.

During photosynthesis a large volume of air passes through the leaf tissues, entering and leaving the leaf through tiny pores called stomata. The air takes out with it a great deal of water vapour, and because of this transpiration loss every plant must draw in, through its roots, much more water than it needs for building up its own tissues.

Plants increase in numbers, and spread from place to place, by means of seeds that ripen from their flowers. The petunia blossom, shown here as an example of a typical flower, has an outer ring of five green sepals that protect it while it is still in bud. These open in summer to expose an inner ring of five brightly coloured petals, united to form a tube, which attract to the flower the bees and other insects that carry pollen. At the heart of the flower are nectaries, which secrete sweet nectar and so encourage each bee to visit many flowers in turn. In some flowers perfume also helps to attract insects. In seeking the hidden nectar, the bee brushes past the ring of five stamens, which are the flower's male organs, and the bee's hairs are dusted with pollen grains from the anthers of these stamens.

When the bee reaches the next flower, some of this pollen is picked up by that flower's female organ, called the pistil, set at the heart of the blossom. Pollen adheres to the sticky stigma at the tip of the pistil, and the pollen grains then grow down within the slender style to the ovary at the base. There, after fertilization, the little ovules, or potential seeds, develop rapidly into ripe seeds within a hard pod that develops from the soft green walls of the ovary. When it is fully ripe this pod splits open, and the fine seeds escape, to be scattered by the wind. Those that alight on bare, moist earth will sprout next spring to send down roots, send up shoots, and eventually develop into fresh petunia plants, so completing the life-cycle.

The annual rhythm of plant growth is caused, in most parts of the world, by seasonal limitations in the warmth or the water supply that is available. Two diagrams that represent different patterns of warmth and rainfall, in different European countries, bring this out.

In the diagram for Zurich, in Switzerland, the blue columns show that there is always ample moisture, all year round. Every month a minimum of 50 millimetres of rain, or its equivalent in the form of snow, falls. But the red curve above this shows that for five months of the year, namely in January, February, the first half of March, the second half of October, November, and December, the average temperature remains below 5° C, which is the practical minimum for plant growth and active life. Therefore, in the Swiss lowland climate, plants grow actively only from mid-March to mid-October, and all kinds must be adapted to survive, in a dormant state, through the winter. The monkshood shown here is a good example of a Swiss plant that grows actively through the summer, storing up food reserves in the large fleshy roots for survival through the cold season. High up in the Alps, the active growing season is shorter still; it may be no more than a few weeks around midsummer.

The second diagram, for Lisbon in Portugal, shows a red

THE CLIMATIC REGIONS OF THE WORLD

Projection: Gall

Scale: 1:92,200,000 equatorial scale

Miles

Kilometres

1 Tropical climates

1a Rainy (humid climate)
   Tropical forest
1b Savanna (humid climate)
   Tropical grassland
1c Highland (humid climate)
   Tropical highland

1d Semi-desert (dry climate)
   Hot semi-desert
1e Desert (dry climate)
   Hot desert

2 Sub-tropical climates

2a Mediterranean
   Scrub woodland, olive etc.
2b Humid
   Deciduous forest

The main vegetation types associated with each climatic region are shown in italics.

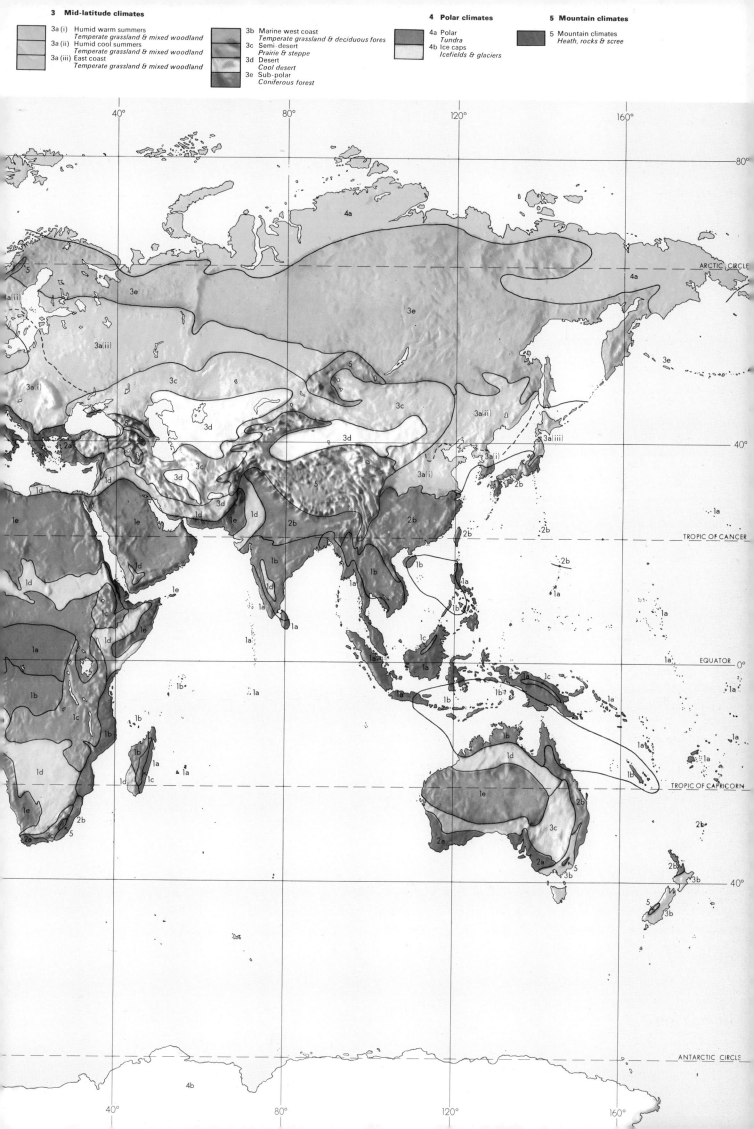

3 Mid-latitude climates

3a (i) Humid warm summers
        Temperate grassland & mixed woodland
3a (ii) Humid cool summers
        Temperate grassland & mixed woodland
3a (iii) East coast
        Temperate grassland & mixed woodland

3b Marine west coast
    Temperate grassland & deciduous fores
3c Semi-desert
    Prairie & steppe
3d Desert
    Cool desert
3e Sub-polar
    Coniferous forest

4 Polar climates

4a Polar
    Tundra
4b Ice caps
    Icefields & glaciers

5 Mountain climates

5 Mountain climates
   Heath, rocks & scree

curve for warmth that never drops below 10°C. Therefore it is never too cold in Lisbon for plants to grow actively. But the blue columns for rainfall fall below the 50-millimetre level during five summer months, from May to September. This is the time when summer heat is greatest and transpiration could, if water were freely available, be most rapid. Rainfall, however, is adequate for plant life only during seven months, from October to April. The plants of Portugal, and all the countries around the Mediterranean Sea, must therefore be adapted to live through an annual spell of summer drought. A characteristic adaptation is a thick fleshy leaf, with a waxy surface to check water-loss, such as is found in the rock rose illustrated here.

These are just two examples of the wide range of limiting seasons that are represented on the map of world climatic regions on pages 14 and 15.

The map of the world's climatic regions brings out the complex pattern of conditions that controls plant life. Each of the great continents holds several climatic regions. Most regions, in their turn, are represented on several continents, though over expanses of land that vary widely in extent and shape. Seasonal patterns of heat and rainfall differ also; those for each continent are described in the chapters that follow.

The broad world picture shows the tropical climates (1) with warmth always adequate for plant growth, grouped on either side of the equator. The rainy tropical climate (1a), which has ample year-round moisture, is limited to relatively small zones in South America, Africa, and coastal districts of India and Indonesia. These carry tall tropical rain forests, with continual growth of great timber trees. In the other humid tropical climates, the savanna (1b) and the highland (1c), the rainfall is seasonal, and most plants show characteristic active and resting spells each year. The typical vegetation pattern is one of occasional trees amid grassland, with scattered clumps of shrubs or tall herbaceous plants. The Guernsey lily is an example of a savanna-zone plant that lives through dry spells as a fleshy, underground bulb. Native to southern Africa, it is grown in the Channel Island from which it derives its name.

In the tropical semi-deserts (1d) all the plants show adaptations to long dry spells, with high potential water-loss under the blazing, almost vertical, rays of the sun. Thanks to occasional rains, specialized plants, such as cacti, aloes, and yuccas, survive on these semi-deserts, but only a very few kinds, such as the stone plants, can exist over the arid true deserts of the tropics (1e), which have no regular wet season and also have great extremes of temperature from day to night.

The subtropical climates (2) include the Mediterranean type (2a) such as that of Lisbon described earlier, with hot dry summers and warm wet winters, characterized by evergreen shrubs adapted to resist summer drought. The Mediterranean climates are found on the west coasts of the continents. On the east coasts are the humid subtropics (2b) which have heavier, though still seasonal, rainfall and support both evergreen and deciduous trees and shrubs and many smaller woodland plants.

Snow and ice   Mosses and lichens

Low herbs and shrubs | Coniferous forests | Deciduous forests | Tropical forests | Snow and ice

← Latitude →

Mosses and lichens

Low herbs and shrubs

Altitude

Coniferous forests

Deciduous forests

Tropical forests

A traveller going south from the North Pole crosses different plant-life zones as he approaches the equator. Increasing warmth and available moisture first permit growth of low plants, then tall conifers, and eventually evergreen tropical forest. If, in the tropics, he ascends a high mountain (far right) this plant-life succession is reversed as he reaches higher and colder zones; above 18,000 feet there is only snow and ice.

In many hot tropical regions rainfall is seasonal, and plants needing constant moisture cannot thrive. The Guernsey lily (left), a typical savanna plant from southern Africa, stores food and moisture through the dry season in its fleshy underground bulb.

In all the mid-latitude climates (3) the winters are so cold that active plant growth ceases for a resting spell. Their humid regions (3a and 3b) carry the characteristic blend of broad-leaved forest and meadow described on the opening pages of the chapter. Towards the colder north of Europe, Asia, and North America, this vegetation changes into evergreen coniferous forest adapted to a shorter growing season. In the drier interior zones of the larger land masses, the grasses of prairies or steppes replace the tall trees. The cool semi-desert (3c) and true deserts (3d) of Central Asia, inland California, Argentina, and Australia support only specialized plants.

In the subpolar climatic region (3e) which runs across Europe, Asia, and North America, the summer period of active growth is so short that only a limited group of plants can survive. Most of these are woody evergreens, ranging from trees such as spruces and pines to lower junipers, heaths, and bilberries, with abundant mosses. Still further north, the region of polar climate (4a) that borders the Arctic Ocean has a summer so brief that only the lowest tundra plants can exist. These are mainly mosses and lichens, including the so-called reindeer "moss" (really a lichen) that sustains wandering reindeer, caribou, and musk oxen. The ground here is continually frozen, just below the surface, in a condition known as permafrost. Finally, the Greenland and Antarctic ice-caps (4b) are too frigid to support any plant life at all.

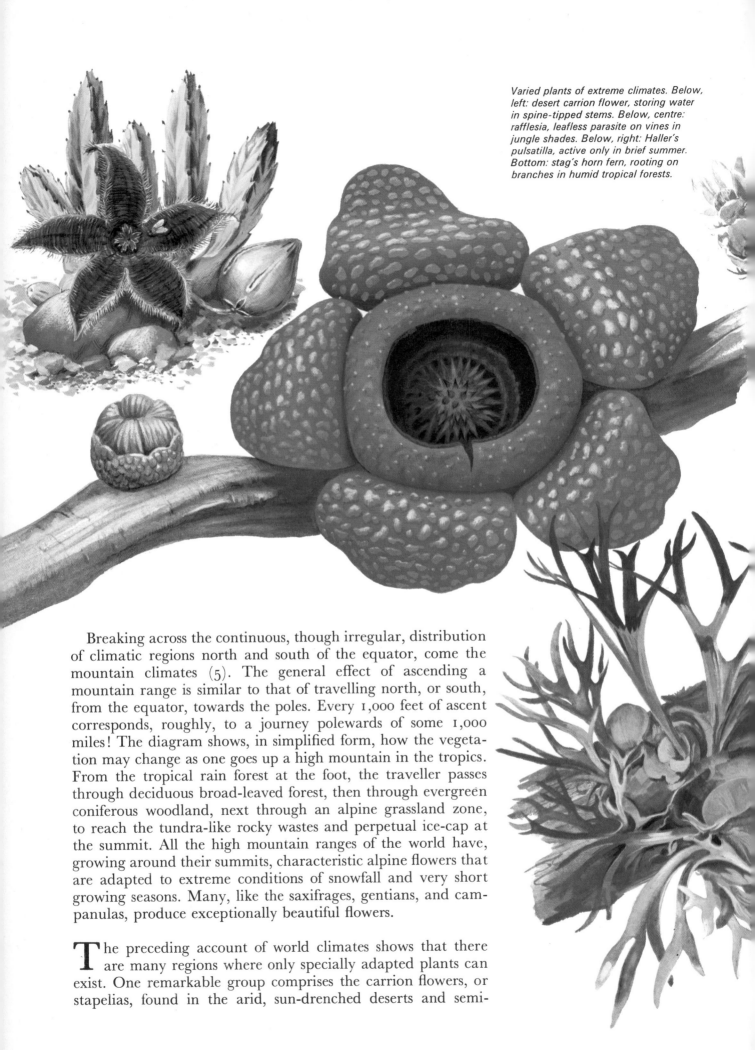

Varied plants of extreme climates. Below, left: desert carrion flower, storing water in spine-tipped stems. Below, centre: rafflesia, leafless parasite on vines in jungle shades. Below, right: Haller's pulsatilla, active only in brief summer. Bottom: stag's horn fern, rooting on branches in humid tropical forests.

Breaking across the continuous, though irregular, distribution of climatic regions north and south of the equator, come the mountain climates (5). The general effect of ascending a mountain range is similar to that of travelling north, or south, from the equator, towards the poles. Every 1,000 feet of ascent corresponds, roughly, to a journey polewards of some 1,000 miles! The diagram shows, in simplified form, how the vegetation may change as one goes up a high mountain in the tropics. From the tropical rain forest at the foot, the traveller passes through deciduous broad-leaved forest, then through evergreen coniferous woodland, next through an alpine grassland zone, to reach the tundra-like rocky wastes and perpetual ice-cap at the summit. All the high mountain ranges of the world have, growing around their summits, characteristic alpine flowers that are adapted to extreme conditions of snowfall and very short growing seasons. Many, like the saxifrages, gentians, and campanulas, produce exceptionally beautiful flowers.

The preceding account of world climates shows that there are many regions where only specially adapted plants can exist. One remarkable group comprises the carrion flowers, or stapelias, found in the arid, sun-drenched deserts and semi-

deserts of southern Africa. These plants have no leaves, all the functions of an ordinary leaf being carried out by thick, fleshy, four-angled stems that bear spines to discourage grazing animals. The stems store the water that the carrion flower's roots gather from infrequent rainstorms. Such stems, having a relatively small surface area, lose less moisture through transpiration than true leaves. The odd, star-shaped flowers open, at the tips of long stalks, close to ground level. Each is patterned in yellow and blood-red to resemble rotting flesh, and gives forth a foul smell like that of carrion. This attracts flesh-eating flies, which carry pollen from one flower to another. Female flies sometimes lay their eggs on carrion flowers, believing they have found real flesh to nourish their brood of maggots, which inevitably starve to death soon after hatching.

Living at the opposite climatic extreme, under constant cold and moisture, the alpine Pasque flowers or pulsatillas open their leaves and blossoms for a short active spell when the snows melt in late spring on the high Alps. They have surprisingly thick woody rootstocks that penetrate deeply into the sparse soil and rocky gravel, and in this they store food reserves, won by their feathery leaves in summer, through the long frozen winter months. Their brilliant flowers quickly attract the earliest insects. Later they ripen fuzzy heads of seeds, each seed having a tuft of hairs to carry it on the wind.

Under the constant rainfall and amid the humid air of the tropical rain forests, many plants contrive to live as epiphytes, supported on the bark and stems of trees instead of on the soil. A remarkable example is the stag's horn fern which grows, in one form or another, in tropical Africa, Madagascar, and eastern Australia. This fern has two forms of leaf. The flat type spreads over the bark of its supporting tree and collects moisture and sodden debris falling from upper branches within the forest. This, along with the fern's own dead leaves, forms a rooting medium for the fern's root system. The other leaf form, which is shaped like the branching antlers of a stag, functions normally, like other green leaves. It also bears the sporophores that produce the wind-borne spores that spread the fern, which is able to thrive under deep shade.

The most remarkable of all the rain-forest plants is the rafflesia of Indonesia, which bears the world's largest flower, often three feet across. This blossom is coloured yellowish-red and has a strong, unpleasant smell which attracts the flesh-eating flies that spread its pollen. Rafflesia is a complete parasite; it has neither leaves nor true roots of its own. Instead its shoots, springing from a seed at ground level, grow along the ground and penetrate those roots of a climbing jungle vine that are on or near the soil surface. The rafflesia taps nourishment and water from the vine, which is itself physically supported by a tall rain-forest tree. Eventually a rafflesia flower bud breaks through the bark of the climber's root, and expands as a single enormous bloom. Since it bears no green leaves, the rafflesia can flourish in the semi-darkness of the jungle floor. The work of photosynthesis that supports it is carried out by its climbing host-plant, perhaps 150 feet overhead!

2 Europe

Vines and olives of warm Mediterranean lands. Bright-flowered rock plants on the high Alps. Oakwoods, meadows, and cornfields of central Europe. Scandinavia's birch and pine forests.

The continent of Europe extends westward from Asia as a series of oddly-shaped peninsulas, separated by large, land-locked seas. To the west lies the broad Atlantic Ocean. The prevailing south-westerly winds that blow over the warm Gulf Stream bring warmth and rain to most of Europe for nearly the whole year round. The seas and broad bays, with their circulating currents, carry this maritime influence far into the heart of the continent. Despite its northerly situation, Europe enjoys a truly temperate climate, which has fitted it well for the development of civilization and culture, aided by the raising of a wide range of plants.

Northern and Central Europe form a great plain or series of low tablelands. This is broken by scattered ranges of high mountains that include the highlands of Norway, Scotland, and Wales, the Pyrenees of France and Spain, the Alps, and the Italian Apennines. The peaks of each high range form islands of mountain or arctic-like climate, and many are snow-clad for most of the year. They influence the local weather but do not upset the equable climate of the continent as a whole. To the south, the land slopes steeply down to the warm, almost land-locked Mediterranean Sea.

Around the Mediterranean the summers are hot and dry, with little rain and ample sunshine. Much rain falls during the cooler winters. Most of the trees and plants that thrive in Portugal, Spain, southern France, Italy, and the Balkans, are specially modified for this climate. They have tough, glossy leaves that resist water loss in summer droughts, and are evergreen so that they can grow actively when rain is available in winter. Mediterranean oaks follow this pattern and resemble giant hollies. One of them, the cork oak of Portugal and Spain,

Autumn in Portugal. In terraced vineyards on hillsides grapes ripen under a strong sun. On the right are cork oaks, stripped of their thick bark. In the foreground some fruits of the season are displayed. From right to left: fig, grapes, fig with olives, and sweet chestnuts with their spiny husk.

develops a very thick bark that seals moisture within the trunk as well as protecting the tree against insects and fungal disease. This bark, or cork layer, can be stripped off without injury to the tree. Once dried in the sun it can be cut in a special way to make bottle stoppers or processed into flooring or insulation sheets. The cork oak is unique among trees in growing fresh bark after each stripping, giving a harvest about every 20 years.

Farmers take advantage of the hot, dry summers of Mediterranean lands by raising grape-vines for fruit and wine. A typical vineyard is situated on a south-facing slope, where it receives maximum sunshine. The land is first laboriously terraced, providing level ground for cultivation, which holds both soil and moisture, and resists erosion. The stony soil and broken rock make effective reservoirs for holding winter moisture within reach of the vine's deep-searching roots. Each vine is skilfully trained to grow on wooden supports, and pruned annually. The soil is kept clean-weeded. The small green flowers ripen by autumn to clusters of green or purple grapes.

For more than 2,000 years olive trees have been a valuable source of food to the Mediterranean peoples. The long-lived olive trees resist drought thanks to their narrow, evergreen, grey-green leaves. Each autumn the familiar olive fruits, holding a hard stone surrounded by tasty green pulp rich in nutritious oil, are gathered by hand. They are either eaten whole, after pickling in salty water, or pressed to extract the oil, which is used for cooking or added to dishes of many kinds.

The wild fig is another drought-resistant tree that has been brought into cultivation as a reliable food resource. Each spring it opens thick, mid-green, lobed leaves that vary remarkably in shape, even on one tree. The fig is not a simple fruit, but a swollen flower-head holding scores of tiny flowers around its central cavity. These are pollinated by little wasps that enter the cavity through the small hole at the tip of the fig.

Another valuable deciduous, broad-leaved tree of this region is the sweet chestnut. It thrives in the foothills where winter cold makes its autumn leaf-fall an advantage. If the leaves were held through the winter, when frost stops water intake from the soil, then the tree would dry out and die. The very large, glossy-surfaced leaves that grow in the spring are adapted to resist summer drought. Its catkins, which open in midsummer and are pollinated by bees, ripen rapidly to yield nutritious nuts. These are delicious when roasted, preserved as marron sweet-meats, or ground to make a meal called polenta.

Characteristic of Mediterranean shores is maquis, a low evergreen woodland or "brush" made up of many varieties of shrubs, including the arbutus, the kermes oak, junipers, and the Judas tree. In western districts grows the cherry laurel, which is often planted in north-west Europe as a hedge or bush. If left unclipped, it bears spikes of white blossoms followed by little black cherries, too bitter for man to eat though attractive to birds. Tall pines thrive along the coast, for their narrow needles and thick bark can resist water-loss. Below them, heaths succeed as dwarf shrubs because their short, narrow leaves are also adapted to retain moisture.

Spring in the Alps. As snow clears from the high slopes, Alpine flowers appear among the rocks. Shown here are crocus, edelweiss (white with yellow centre), blue gentian, and purple mountain saxifrage. Beyond the rugged, cone-bearing pines, larchwoods appear on far hillsides.

EUROPE
(North Europe)

© Geographical Projects

Ice caps	Deciduous forest
Tundra	Temperate grassland
Mountain	Prairie
Coniferous forest	Desert
	Semi-desert

Projection: Azimuthal Equidistant

Scale: 1:11,100,000

Miles
0 50 100 150 200 250 300 350

Kilometres
0 50 100 150 200 250 300 350 400 450 500 550 600

Barley	Bluebell
Beech	Broad bean
Beetroot	Buttercup
Bilberry	Cabbage
Birch	Chicory

ARCTIC CIRCLE

66°   24°   16°   8°   0°   8°   16°   24°

N O R W E G I A N   S E A

These plants occur everywhere south of this boundary

FAEROE IS.

SHETLAND IS.

ORKNEY IS.

58°
16°

A T L A N T I C   O C E A N

BRITISH ISLES

IRISH SEA

N O R T H   S E A

GULF OF BOTHNIA

Lake Vänern

GOTLAND

BORNHOLM

B A L T I C   S E A

G OF FIN

50°

ENGLISH CHANNEL

8°

BAY OF BISCAY

Loire

Rhine

Elbe

Vistula

Danube

0°   8°   16°   24°

Clover
Cocksfoot grass
Crocus
Edelweiss
Flag iris
Flax

Foxglove
Gentian
Hawthorn
Hazel
Heather
Hemlock plant

Holly
Hop
Ivy
Juniper
Larch
Mistletoe

Mushroom
Oak
Oat
Pasture grass
Pine
Reed

Reed-mace
Saxifrage
Spruce
Sweet chestnut
Thistle
Vine

Wheat
White water lily
Wild daffodil
Wild raspberry
Wild rose
Willow herb

To the north of the Mediterranean region the Alps, Europe's highest mountains, rise to a general height of 10,000 feet, and create their own climatic zone. Similar "alpine" conditions are found along other great European ranges, such as the Pyrenees. The mountain summits are covered with ice and snow all year round, and in winter the valleys also are frostbound. Direction of slope influences both climate and plant life; trees and crops grow at higher altitudes on warm, south-facing slopes than on cold, north-facing ones. The spring thaw, which starts in April, moves slowly up the slopes, freeing pastures and meadows from their snowy covering. On higher ground, the screes of gravel and the broken rock-faces are warm enough to support plant life for only a few months in summer. Only the true alpine plants survive here. Many form low tufts or carpets of evergreen foliage, that persist despite burial by snow. In the brief, bright, late spring they put forth brilliant flowers and then quickly ripen seeds that scatter over the bare soil before winter snows return.

The purple saxifrage grows on a few high Scottish mountains as well as in the Alps, and forms mats of tough evergreen leaves on trailing stems, resistant to the soil movement caused by frost. It opens beautiful bell-shaped blossoms in May. In rock crevices many kinds of gentians open intensely blue flowers to attract the pollinating insects that live around the summits. Other plants pass the long winter as bulbs or corms. These include the spring crocus, which bears cup-shaped blue or white flowers within a tuft of narrow green leaves.

At high altitudes grows the edelweiss, a low plant adapted to extreme conditions and a very short growing season. Its leaves, borne in star-shaped clusters, are clad in white hairs that check water-loss, helping it to survive in rock crevices under the bright sunshine.

Trees, too, are specially modified for this extreme climate. The larch, which grows at higher altitudes than other timber trees, bears narrow needles resistant to water-loss. Unlike other conifers it loses its foliage completely in winter. Larch has an exceptionally tough timber, and its shoots grow vigorously again even when the tree has been seriously damaged by snowbreak, gales, or avalanches.

North of the Alps the great plain of northern Europe stretches from the Atlantic coast of France eastwards to Russia and the Ural mountains, including in its climatic range the British Isles and southern Scandinavia. Its summers are hot and sunny, with ample rain in the west but extreme heat and drought to the east. The winters, mild in the west, become progressively harsher towards the east, where snow and ice grip the land from December to late March.

The plants best suited to this climate are the deciduous broad-leaved trees. These develop a large active crown of foliage very quickly in the spring. Before human settlement began, the north European plain was one vast oak forest, with beech, ash, and sycamore on limestone hills, and alder and willow in marshy valleys. Occasional gaps in this forest were

Far right: three woody plants of forest fringes: wild rose, wild raspberry, and hazel, bearing delicious nuts.

EUROPE
(South Europe)

© Geographical Projects

Mountain		Mediterranean	
Coniferous forest		Savanna	
Deciduous forest		Desert	
Temperate grassland		Semi-desert	
Prairie		Fertile lands	

Projection: Azimuthal Equidistant

Scale: 1:11,100,000

Miles
0 50 100 150 200 250 300 350

Kilometres
0 50 100 150 200 250 300 350 400 450 500 550 600

Barley

Beech

Beetroot

Bilberry

Birch

Bluebell

Broad bean

Buttercup

Cabbage

Cherry laurel

Chicory

Clover

Cocksfoot grass

Crocus

ATLANTIC OCEAN

BAY OF BISCAY

Iberian Peninsula

Tagus

Douro

Ebro

STR. OF GIBRALTAR

Loire

Rhône

Rhine

Elbe

Danube

ALPS

APENNINES

CORSICA

SARDINIA

BALEARIC IS.

TYRRHENIAN SEA

ADRIATIC SEA

SICILY

MEDITERRANEAN

These plants occur everywhere north of this boundary

Edelweiss
Evergreen oak
Fig
Flag iris
Flax
Foxglove

Gentian
Hawthorn
Hazel
Heather
Hemlock plant
Holly

Hop
Ivy
Juniper
Larch
Mistletoe
Mushroom

Oak
Oat
Olive
Pasture grass
Pine
Reed

Reed-mace
Saxifrage
Spruce
Sweet chestnut
Thistle
Vine

Wheat
White water lily
Wild daffodil
Wild raspberry
Wild rose
Willow herb

colonized by tall, perennial grasses that grew, flowered, and seeded in the warm summers, and passed the frozen winters as rootstocks beneath the snow. The northward spread of civilization was based on clearance of woodland to extend these natural meadows.

Oak, the leading tree, owes its dominance to long life and a large seed, the acorn, which gives a sturdy seedling able to shoot up through grass and weeds. Oak timber proved an invaluable resource for European farmers and seamen, for its heartwood is naturally durable and very strong, yet easily shaped by hand tools into beams for houses and hulls for ships.

Low-flowering plants that spring from winter bulbs flourish in the more open, broad-leaved woodlands, particularly those of oak and ash. They pass the cold winter deep down within the soil, and in spring send up vigorous tufts of leaves to make use of sunshine before the trees above them cast a leafy shade. Their gay flowers open then, and as summer advances they ripen their seed-pods. Meanwhile the leaves, now over-shaded, wither and send down food reserves to the underground bulb, ready for next year's growing season. Among the most attractive of wild bulbs is the rather rare and local daffodil. Early in May, the more widespread bluebell, *Endymion non-scriptus,* forms seas of brilliant blue flowers on the floors of oakwoods and similar open broad-leaved woodland throughout western Europe.

On lime-rich soils, over chalk or limestone rocks, beech takes the place of oak as the leading forest tree. It has smooth grey bark and oval leaves, and bears triangular brown nuts that are eaten by mice, squirrels, and birds. Beech nuts, like acorns, were once a main food for the swine that ranged the forests in autumn. Beech yields a strong timber which, though not durable out of doors, makes sound furniture and many other everyday wooden things, including spoons, bowls, platters, and even shoes such as clogs or sabots.

Beech casts a very dense shade. Few other trees or plants can live beneath it, but when old trees do die and fall, many shrubs and flowering plants colonize the clearings. Hazel, which grows from a large round nut, forms a spreading bush that bears hanging "lamb's tail" male catkins on leafless branches in spring. Its female catkins, seldom noticed, are leafy buds with a tuft of crimson stigmas. The supple hazel stems can be woven into light, yet tough, wooden screens. Such hurdles formed the wattles of "wattle-and-daub" walls used in mediaeval houses, the daub consisting of a coating of clay.

In the rich soil and half-shade of the beechwood edge, the wild raspberry flourishes. Each spring it sends up a slender cane bearing prickles that protect it from grazing animals. In the summer of the following year this cane bears white flowers and then juicy red fruits. Once these have ripened, it dies, but already another cane has sprung up, from the underground rootstock, to succeed it. The wild rose has a longer-lived, tougher stem that carries sharp, strong prickles to discourage browsing deer. One of the ancestors of the beautiful briar roses cultivated in gardens, it bears pink blossoms, followed in autumn by bright red oval fruits called hips. Both rose hips and

Some crops and weeds native to Europe, all shown at flowering or fruiting stage. They are not drawn to scale. Above: barley with its bearded seed-head, and the broad bean that ripens nutritious seeds in long pods. Centre, left: the spear, or bull, thistle, with sharp spines to check grazing animals, and yellow meadow buttercup, defended by its bitter taste. The field mushroom, another pasture plant, draws nourishment from decaying organic matter.

Centre, right: blue-flowered flax, source of linen fibre and linseed, with chicory, which is grown either for the coffee substitute made from its roots or as a tender white vegetable. Right: hops, the fruit heads of a climbing vine-like plant, which are used as a flavouring for bitter beer.

raspberries attract berry-eating birds that carry their seeds to fresh clearings.

The foxglove is a biennial, or two-year plant, that exploits the rich soil of new gaps in woodlands, particularly those of beech. In its first year it grows from seed into a low tuft of leaves with a strong root. The following year it sends up a tall flowering shoot, sometimes six feet tall, that carries a dense head of drooping purple blossoms, each shaped like the finger of a glove. These ripen to pods holding thousands of tiny seeds, so small that they are scattered by winds throughout the woods.

The rosebay willow herb, so called because its slender leaves resemble those of many willows, has the same life cycle as the foxglove and grows in similar woodland clearings. It bears, in its second year, masses of rosy-mauve flowers, each made up of five separate petals with a central ovary. When this ripens in autumn it releases a cloud of tiny seeds, each bearing a tuft of white hairs that support it on the wind as it drifts to new ground. Because it colonizes burnt-over land, it is also called the "fireweed."

Plants from all the temperate regions of the world are now cultivated on fields won from the forests that once clothed the European lowlands. But there are also many native crop plants that, before the later introductions, supported civilization on the continent of Europe. One of these is barley, a leading cereal that can usually be recognized by the long hairs on its seed-heads, although some wheats bear long hairs too. Barley is rich in carbohydrates, and although it does not make good bread, it is valuable for fattening beef cattle. Beer is made from barley by germinating the grain so that part of its food reserves, originally starch, are first converted into sugar. They are then fermented into alcohol.

In order to add nutritious protein to their diet, European farmers have, from the earliest times, raised plants of the sweet-pea family, or Leguminoseae. These have nodules on their roots that "fix" nitrogen from the air, so converting an inert gas into a useful plant food. The broad bean is a characteristic large-seeded legume; others are peas and lentils. The broad bean bears typical compound leaves and white flowers with three broad upper petals, called the "standard" and the "wings," that attract pollinating bees. The two lower petals, folded together in the "keel," oblige the bee to brush past the stamens and stigma within them as it penetrates to the inner nectary, so aiding cross-fertilization. Broad beans, which develop within a typical pod, are eaten in their green state as a fresh, cooked vegetable, or allowed to ripen and then fed as hard fodder to cattle and horses.

Lacking cotton, the early Europeans grew the flax plant to gain the strong vegetable fibre called linen, which can be bleached white and woven into fine durable cloth. Flax is a slender annual plant with narrow leaves and bright blue flowers.

Top scene: two salt-tolerant seashore plants that are ancestors of major crops (seen cultivated beyond). Wild beetroot (left) gave us red beet, sugar beet, and mangolds. From wild cabbage (right) farmers developed cauliflower, Brussels sprouts, and kale.

Lower scene: many waterside plants thrive only when rooted in sodden, fertile mud. By this English river grow yellow flag iris, poisonous, white-flowered hemlock, and reed-mace, or bulrush, which bears decorative seed-heads.

These ripen to seed-pods holding oily brown seeds, called linseed—the source of the linseed oil used in paints. To prepare linen, however, the plants are pulled from the ground before they flower, and their stems are then "retted" by steeping them in water to loosen the softer tissues, which are removed by drying and beating. The tough, pale fibres remaining are spun and woven into cloth.

Before coffee and tea had been introduced, Europeans flavoured their drinks with various herbs. One that has survived in regular use today is chicory. This is a biennial plant with a blue flower shaped like a double daisy. In its first year it forms a thick white rootstock, which is gathered, roasted, and ground to make a fair substitute for coffee. Alternatively the rootstock can be replanted and forced in a dark hothouse to give a tasty white salad vegetable. The hop is another herb raised as a flavouring for drink. It imparts a bitter taste to beer. It is a climbing plant with a perennial rootstock, and under cultivation its slender green stems are trained up strings supported by wires strung from poles. In the autumn the hop-vines are harvested either by hand or by machines that strip off the female flowers. These are soaked in water to wash out the precious flavour.

The meadows, pastures, and cornfields of Europe are often so invaded by weeds that the farmer finds it impossible to eradicate them completely. The yellow buttercup, for example, persists in pastures because its poisonous leaves have an acid taste, and cows leave it alone when they graze grass beside it. It spreads by numerous hard seeds and persists through the winter as a tough root in the turf. Thistles, which are spread over long distances by their small, wind-blown seeds, are also avoided by most animals because of their sharp spines, although donkeys will eat them.

On well-grazed pastures edible mushrooms, *Agaricus campestris*, spring up. When mushroom spores alight on ground soiled by dung they germinate and develop thin white threads running through the soil. Eventually this mass of threads sends up a large spore-bearing body, which is the mushroom we eat.

On the sandy seashores of Europe grows the wild beet, or beetroot, a biennial plant adapted to withstand the salty soil. After one year's growth from seed, it forms a stout root in which it stores food reserves, not as starch, but in the unusual form of sugar. Cultivators have developed two valuable crops from this source, the red beetroot eaten as a vegetable and the white sugar beet, which supports the European sugar industry. Another seashore plant is the wild cabbage. Its fleshy leaves and stalks store nourishment through the winter months. Under cultivation this small and straggly herb has been developed into many varieties, such as red cabbage and spring cabbage with edible leaves; kohlrabi with a fleshy, swollen stem; cauliflower with delicious flower buds, and Brussels sprout with tasty side buds.

Running streams, bringing a constant supply of water and nutrients carried in silt, enable tall herbs to flourish along their

A lakeside scene in north-east Scotland, with pines and silver birch trees. In the background the hillslopes are coloured by purple flowers of heather. Margin shows Scots pine foliage (top), female flowers (at tip) and ripening cones; birch foliage (centre), with upright female catkins, drooping male ones; and bilberry (bottom), bearing fruit.

banks. Most of these live through the winter as rootstocks in the mud, which is often frozen below ice. The flag iris bears handsome yellow blossoms in May, and in midsummer white clusters of blossom open on the hemlock, a tall poisonous plant with purple spots on its green stem. In autumn the reed-mace, sometimes called the bulrush or cat-tail, ripens long, dark-brown seed-heads that are often gathered for decoration.

The northern part of the great European plain, from Scotland and Scandinavia across north Russia to the Ural Mountains, has its own vegetational pattern of short-season trees and low, woody shrubs. Birch is the characteristic tree, and its dwarf race grows farther north than any other. In the warmth of the short northern spring it sends out a multitude of small leaves, strung along thin twigs so that they make full use of bright sunshine during the very long summer days. At this season its white bark helps to keep the growing trunk cool, since it reflects heat rays. Birch bears male and female catkins in spring. The latter ripen in autumn and scatter myriads of tiny wind-borne seeds.

The traditional grain crop of these northern countries is the oat, which ripens its grain during a growing season shorter than that needed by most other cereals. Oats do not make good bread, but oatcakes and oatmeal porridge are nutritious foods, and both grain and foliage are used as fodder for farm stock.

Despite their short growing seasons in the north, two ever-green conifers, spruce and pine, form vast forests that are a major world resource of timber. Pines take two years to ripen their cones, but spruce cones mature in six months. Both kinds hold winged seeds that the winds scatter in spring.

On the forest floor, and far north into the tundra beyond the tree limit, grow dwarf evergreen shrubs with tough, wiry stems and roots that withstand the freezing and thawing of the soil. Heather and similar heaths grow slowly in the short summers. Their soft shoots are browsed by deer, including reindeer, and clipped by grouse and ptarmigan. In autumn they open bright purple flowers in short spikes and quickly ripen many tiny seeds. The bilberry, which opens a pink, waxy, bell-shaped flower in midsummer, ripens juicy, black autumn berries, delicious to eat, which attract the birds that spread its seeds.

The cold true tundra region, with little vegetation except low mosses and lichens that yield food for roving reindeer, extends along the Arctic shores of north-east Europe and also down the Scandinavian mountain chain. Contrasting with the tundra in terms of climate but equally as desolate is the semi-desert region north of the Caspian Sea, in the far south-east of Europe. Here only drought-resistant plants such as glasswort and tamarisk can survive.

3 Asia

Ricefields and jungles of tropical Asia. Himalayan cedars, primulas, and rhododendrons. Siberian sprucewoods, and cold northern tundras. Peaches, poppies, and hyacinths of the warm south-west.

At the heart of the vast continent of Asia the mighty Himalayas and their neighbouring mountain ranges form a barrier between four contrasting climatic regions. The cold north extends across Siberia, the hot south down into India and Indonesia. To the west, a warm, dry region, with sparse winter rains, runs through Iran to Turkey. To the east, a moister sub-tropical zone extends across China to Japan.

Every summer the central land mass of Asia, which includes the great Gobi desert, heats up. The resulting low air-pressure draws in moisture-laden south-westerly winds across the Indian Ocean. When these reach the uplands they rise and shed their moisture in torrential monsoon rains. South-east Asia is therefore hot all the year round, but has contrasting dry and rainy seasons.

Rice, the food grain that supports millions of people in tropical Asia, was originally a riverside grass, adapted to these monsoon conditions. An annual, it sprang up from seed on mudbanks and grew steadily taller as the floodwaters rose. When the rivers subsided, it ripened its seeds, which became scattered over the dry banks to await next year's floods. Asian farmers cultivate rice by following the same cycle, first sowing seed in nurseries on damp mud, then transplanting the shoots to paddy-fields. These are flooded by monsoon rainwater diverted from streams, but are drained later when the crop has developed seed-heads. At harvest-time, about six months after the germination of the seed, the ears are cut with a sickle and the grain is threshed out.

Other plants respond to the rhythm of the monsoons by various patterns of growth and form. The lotus, a water lily growing in lakes and deep streams, can adjust the length of its

Ricefields in Indonesia. Flat fields flooded by monsoon rains are ploughed by buffaloes and then the rice plants are planted singly by hand. Bananas (right) are cultivated around villages. In the jungles grow the evergreen rubber plant (bottom left) and dendrobium orchids, here seen rooting on a teak log. The sacred lotus flourishes in slow streams.

stems to meet floods. Some of its leaves float on the surface, but others stand clear of the water. The curved outlines of the leaves, and the beautiful cup-shaped lotus blossom figure frequently in sacred Hindu and Buddhist art.

The tree-like banana that grows wild in the jungles of tropical Asia is really a huge soft-stemmed plant with a tough underground stem that carries it safely through the dry season. When the rains come, it sends up a stout shoot composed of thick leaf-stalks set one within another, each ending in a huge oblong leaf blade. Through the centre of this stem the long flower-stalk ascends, emerges, and bends over. It carries around its sides many bunches of female flowers that later ripen to the familiar banana fruits, while near its tip grow the male flowers that provide pollen for fertilization.

A shrub adapted to continuous growth through both wet and dry seasons is the rubber plant, *Ficus elastica,* which must not be confused with the South American rubber tree. Its thick, leathery, dark-green leaves resist water-loss during the dry season. If the plant is injured it exudes a white milky sap that hardens to a rubbery substance, as a protection against insect attack.

Many of the tall trees of the monsoon region lose their leaves during the dry season and grow taller and stouter only during the rains. This produces annual rings throughout their timber, in common with trees growing in temperate climates, but in contrast to trees growing under constant heat and rainfall. The best known of these monsoon-region trees is teak, a magnificent tree growing 150 feet tall, and up to 40 feet round, that bears large heart-shaped leaves, tiny white flowers, and large seeds. It yields a very strong, naturally durable, golden-brown timber that is exported from Burma and Thailand to all parts of the world.

The beautiful dendrobium orchid is one of many epiphytes that thrive in the monsoon forests. In the rainy season, it puts forth shoots with pale-green leaves, some evergreen, some deciduous, and opens delicate, highly coloured flowers to attract insects. During the dry spell it rests, conserving moisture in its bulbous stem. The banyan, one of the most spectacular of Asiatic trees, also begins life as an epiphyte. It sprouts from a seed dropped on to the branch of a tree by a passing bird. As the banyan develops, it sends down an aerial root that takes hold in the soil. Becoming well established, it grows horizontal branches that, in turn, send down more aerial roots. Eventually one banyan may become a grove of interlocked stems and branches.

Thousands of years ago the people of tropical Asia began to cultivate strong-tasting wild plants as spices to flavour their monotonous diet of rice. The best known and widely used of these spices, pepper, grows as a vine twining around upright supports. It bears oval leaves and strings of red peppercorns, which turn black after picking. Another familiar Asiatic spice, nutmeg, is the seed of a small evergreen tree native to Indonesia. Green, bell-shaped flowers give way to yellow, plum-shaped fruits that contain the nutmeg kernels. The dried pulp of the

The evergreen mango tree (above) is grown in Indian gardens for its luscious fruits. Hibiscus bushes (inset) are cultivated for their bright flowers, of varied colours, which open throughout the year. Jute (outline below) is grown in flooded fields for its tough-fibred stems.

Near right: two Indonesian spices. Pepper is raised as a vine; the black peppercorn is extracted from its soft berries. Nutmegs ripen as hard seeds.

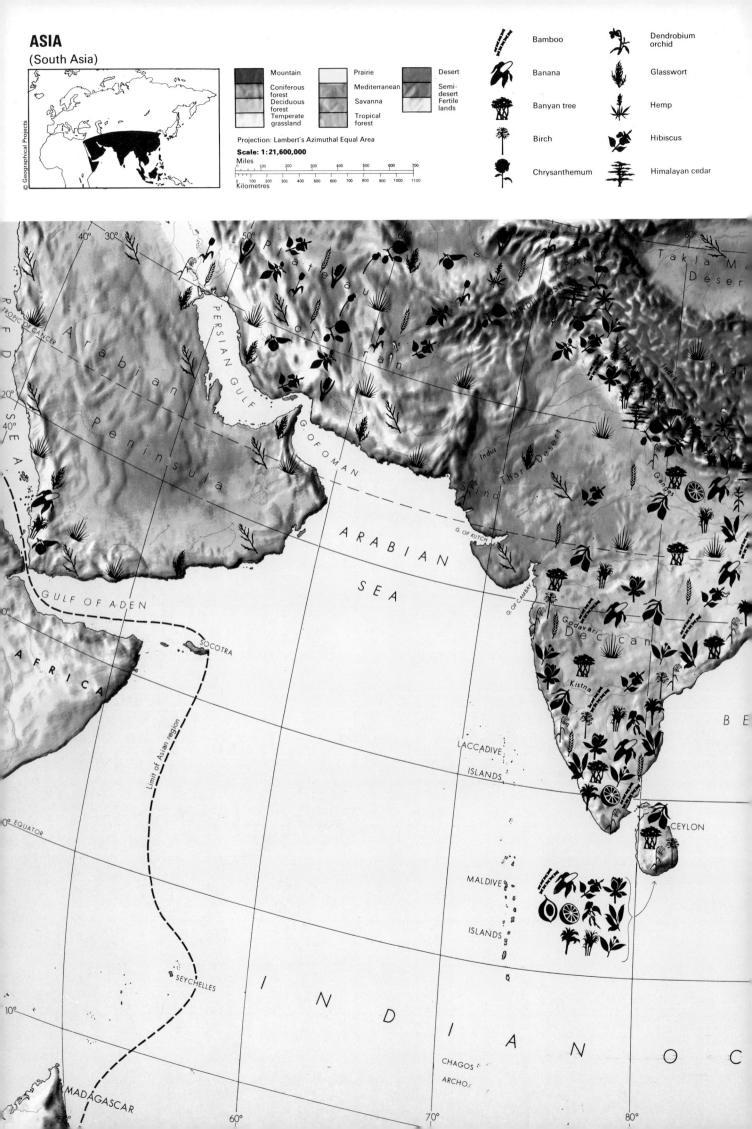

ASIA
(South Asia)

© Geographical Projects

Mountain	Prairie	Desert
Coniferous forest	Mediterranean	Semi-desert
Deciduous forest	Savanna	Fertile lands
Temperate grassland	Tropical forest	

Projection: Lambert's Azimuthal Equal Area

Scale: 1:21,600,000

Miles
0 100 200 300 400 500 600 700

Kilometres
0 100 200 300 400 500 600 700 800 900 1000 1100

Bamboo

Banana

Banyan tree

Birch

Chrysanthemum

Dendrobium orchid

Glasswort

Hemp

Hibiscus

Himalayan cedar

TROPIC OF CANCER

RED SEA

Arabian Peninsula

PERSIAN GULF

Plateau of Iran

HINDU KUSH

PAMIR

Takla Makan Desert

Himalaya

Indus

Plat

G. OF OMAN

Sind

Thar Desert

Indus

Ganges

G. OF KUTCH

G. OF CAMBAY

ARABIAN SEA

GULF OF ADEN

AFRICA

SOCOTRA

Limit of Asian region

Deccan

Godavari

Kistna

B E

LACCADIVE ISLANDS

EQUATOR

CEYLON

SEYCHELLES

MALDIVE ISLANDS

INDIAN OCEAN

CHAGOS ARCHOS.

MADAGASCAR

Himalayan primula
Hyacinth
Japanese ced
Juniper
Jute

Lotus
Maidenhair tree
Mango
Mulberry
Nutmeg

Opium poppy
Orange
Pasture grass
Peach
Pepper

Pine
Rhododendron
Rice
Rubber plant
Sago palm

Spruce
Sugar cane
Tamarisk
Tea
Teak

Tulip
Walnut
Wheat

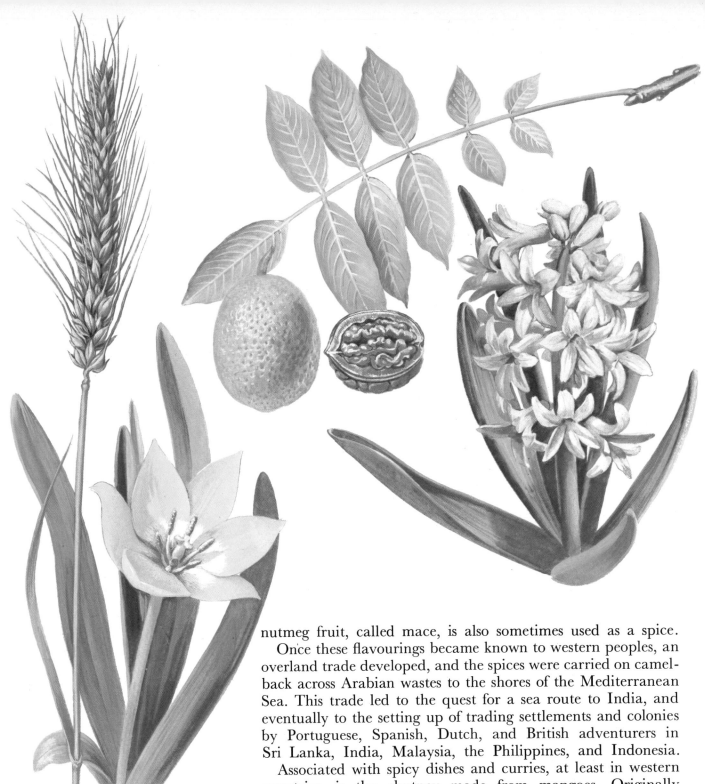

In Turkey, warm summers favour the growth of short-season plants, dormant for most of the year. Wheat (above) is a vigorous annual grass that in the wild passes the winter as a large food-packed seed; hence its widespread cultivation by man. The walnut tree (top centre) rapidly develops a large, nutritious, oily seed. Tulip (above) and hyacinth (above right) open sturdy leaves and gay flower-spikes each spring, but then wither. They pass the hot summer and cold winter as underground bulbs.

nutmeg fruit, called mace, is also sometimes used as a spice.

Once these flavourings became known to western peoples, an overland trade developed, and the spices were carried on camel-back across Arabian wastes to the shores of the Mediterranean Sea. This trade led to the quest for a sea route to India, and eventually to the setting up of trading settlements and colonies by Portuguese, Spanish, Dutch, and British adventurers in Sri Lanka, India, Malaysia, the Philippines, and Indonesia.

Associated with spicy dishes and curries, at least in western countries, is the chutney made from mangoes. Originally native to India, Burma, and Malaysia, mangoes are now cultivated throughout tropical Asia, where they are relished as fresh, juicy fruits. They are borne on tall evergreen trees that have slender leaves and sprays of pinkish-white flowers.

Hibiscus is the typical flowering shrub of the Asiatic tropics, where it takes the place of the rose grown in temperate lands. Its large trumpet-shaped flowers spring freely and repeatedly from a shapely base of wavy-leaved foliage, except for a brief dormant spell in the dry season. The blossoms vary in shade from white to pink or blue.

Of the many tropical Asiatic plants that are now grown as crops in many regions of the world, one of the most commercially important is sugar cane. Sugar cane is a large bamboo-like grass that builds up rich food reserves during its period of

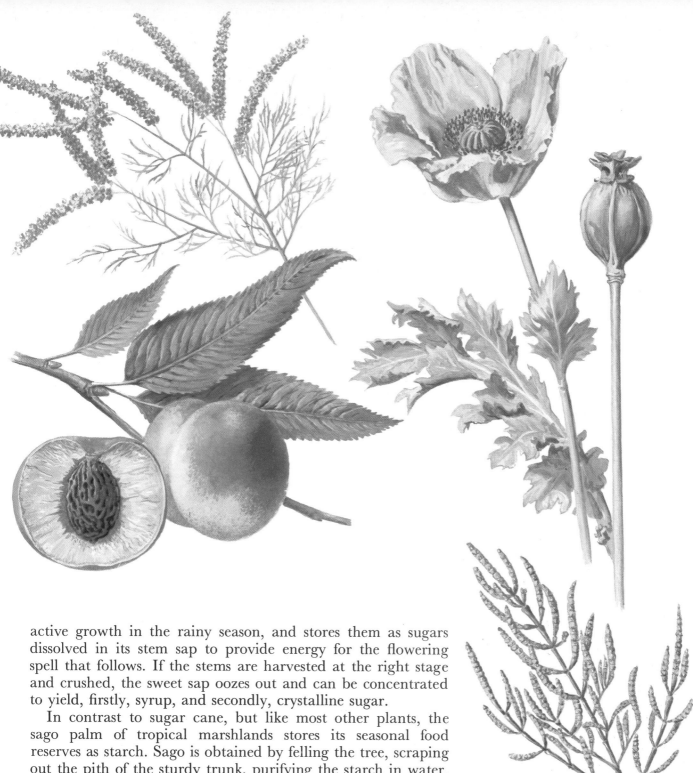

active growth in the rainy season, and stores them as sugars dissolved in its stem sap to provide energy for the flowering spell that follows. If the stems are harvested at the right stage and crushed, the sweet sap oozes out and can be concentrated to yield, firstly, syrup, and secondly, crystalline sugar.

In contrast to sugar cane, but like most other plants, the sago palm of tropical marshlands stores its seasonal food reserves as starch. Sago is obtained by felling the tree, scraping out the pith of the sturdy trunk, purifying the starch in water, and heating it to make it coagulate into granules.

On the flat flood plains of river deltas of tropical Asia, especially the delta of the River Ganges near Calcutta, peasant farmers cultivate the tall tropical plant that produces the coarse fibre called jute. The farmers sow the seed densely and harvest the stems when they have grown ten feet tall, just before the yellow blossoms open. They soak the stems in water, then beat them on the surface to free the soft tissues, leaving the tough, long fibres ready for drying.

Most of south-west Asia, between the Himalayas and the Mediterranean, Black, and Caspian seas, forms a region of low rainfall, with cold winters and hot, dry summers. Plant life depends on seasonal rains, and everything that grows here is adapted in some way to survive long spells of drought. An

The peach tree (above left), which grows in Iran, opens bright pink blossoms on leafless twigs in March, followed by long dark-green leaves and soft-skinned fruits, each holding a large stony seed within luscious pulp. Opium poppy (top right) has fleshy leaves with grey waxy surfaces that resist drought. An annual, it persists by ripening hundreds of tiny seeds. On arid lands near the Caspian Sea, the bushy tamarisk (top left) bears minute leaves to resist drought. The leafless glasswort (above) stores water from salty soils in swollen stems.

ASIA
(North Asia)

© Geographical Projects

Ice caps	Deciduous forest	Savanna
Tundra	Temperate grassland	Desert
Mountain	Prairie	Semi-desert
Coniferous forest	Mediterranean	Fertile lands

Projection: Lambert's Azimuthal Equal Area

Scale: 1:21,600,000

Miles
0   100   200   300   400   500   600   700

Kilometres
0   100 200 300 400 500 600 700 800 900 1000 1100

	Bamboo		Dryas plant
	Birch		Glasswort
	Chrysanthemum		Hemp
	Dwarf willow		Hibiscus

50°
-10°
60°
70°
ARCTIC CIRCLE
ARC
30°
SPITSBERGEN
40°
FRANZ JOSEF LAND
50°
60°

0°
BARENTS SEA
NOVAYA ZEMLYA

E
U
R
O
P
E

BALTIC SEA
GULF OF BOTHNIA
10°
Lake Ladoga
Lake Onega
URAL MOUNTAINS
Siberia
Ob
Plain

Volga

20°
Danube
Limit of Asian region
Ob

BLACK SEA
Don
Volga
CAUCASUS
Limit of Asian region

30°
MEDITERRANEAN SEA
CASPIAN SEA
ARAL SEA
Lake Balkhash
Syr Darya

30°
Euphrates
Arabian Peninsula
Plateau of Iran
Amu Darya
PAMIR
Tarim
Takla Makan

40°
50°
60°
70°
80°

Himalayan cedar
Hyacinth
Japanese cedar
Juniper

Maidenhair tree
Mulberry
Opium poppy
Orange

Pasture grass
Peach
Pine
Rhododendron

Rhubarb
Rice
Sphagnum moss
Spruce

Tamarisk
Tea
Tulip
Walnut

Wheat

extremely adverse habitat is found in the salty deserts around the land-locked Caspian and Aral seas. Here a blazing sun concentrates common salt in an arid soil, and only specially adapted plants, called halophytes, can survive. One is the soft, shrubby glasswort, so-called because its ash was used as a source of the soda needed by mediaeval glassmakers. During droughts it stores water in its fleshy, jointed stems, which have waxy surfaces to check transpiration. Another halophyte is the tamarisk, a woody bush bearing a name derived from the Hebrew word for a sweeping broom. Its brush-like foliage of needle-shaped leaves loses little moisture during droughts, and it draws soil water through remarkably long roots—up to 50 yards long! In other parts of the world these plants grow only on salt marshes and seaside sand dunes.

Wheat is the main food grain cultivated on the better soils of this region. Cultivated wheat has been developed from an annual grass that draws on spring rains for rapid growth. The grass flowers and then, under the summer sun, ripens a large seed-head, or ear. When this breaks up, the individual seeds lie dormant on dry soil until the next spring. The earliest Stone-Age cultivators of Iran began to harvest ripe ears of wheat in about 7500 B.C., storing them for making bread, and sowing only a fraction for the next year's crop. Thus wheat became a staple food and was carried, first to Europe, later to almost every country in the world with a climate suitable for its growth.

Often found among wheat grains are the small seeds of the opium poppy, another annual, semi-desert plant native to south-west Asia. Under cultivation it yields poppy seeds for confectionery and for poppy-seed oil. If the seed-pods are scratched, a milky juice, rich in potent alkaloids, exudes and solidifies. This waxy solid is collected and refined to produce the opium and morphine drugs that are used medicinally to deaden pain, but is also smoked in the crude state as a dangerous narcotic.

Many plants of this region form underground bulbs to enable them to survive both the cold winter and the hot dry summer. The wild tulips and hyacinths found here have an extremely short active season. The warmth and moisture of spring enables them to send up green leaves, flower, and form seeds, but their stalks wither in the summer heat and they remain dormant through the cold winter as bulbs.

The wild peach, native to Iran, stores its food reserves in its trunk, and puts forth pink blossoms in March, before its dark-green leaves expand. The soft-fleshed fruit, surrounding a hard stone that checks seed-eating creatures, ripens through the summer heat. Walnut, another widely-planted food tree, which originates in Turkey, does not open its compound leaves and quaint male and female catkins until May. By late summer the ripening nuts have fallen and their outer green husks are rotting away.

Southern China and Japan have a warm temperate climate influenced by the south-western monsoons that blow in from the China seas, bringing ample summer rains. Bamboo,

Left: the majestic Himalayan cedar forms vast evergreen forests along the Himalayan foothills; note barrel-shaped cones. Beneath it grow shrubby rhododendrons, with thick glossy leaves and bunches of brilliant flowers. On the woodland floor is the Himalayan primula; its single upright flower stalk is topped by a rosette of blossoms.

the characteristic plant of the region, is a giant woody stemmed grass capable of growing with fantastic speed in wet seasons. Its shoots, which are sometimes eaten as a cooked vegetable, can grow 15 inches a day! It survives dry spells in a dormant state, by storing food in its huge rootstock. Bamboos produce feathery flowers. Some varieties flower only once in their lifetime, after growing for many years. After seeding, the whole clump dies and the thickets are renewed by seedlings. Bamboo stalks are used for building, tools, and weapons, and constitute a major resource for oriental peasant life.

China is the homeland of the wild orange tree, a drought resistant evergreen with dark-green, waxy foliage, white flowers, each with five petals, and the familiar juicy fruits, with oily skins. The orange's high food value and delicious flavour have led to its cultivation in all subtropical lands.

In south-eastern China the quaint maidenhair tree, *Ginkgo biloba,* survives in a few wild groves. Named from its resemblance to the maidenhair fern, this tree is one of the world's oldest in the scale of evolution. Fossil forms are found in rock deposits over 200 million years old. The pale-green triangular leaves, with parallel veins and a notch at the tip, make recognition easy. Their beauty has led to the widespread cultivation of the maidenhair tree in oriental temple gardens, western parks, and as a street tree in the United States. Male trees bear green catkins, while females have plum-like fruits with hard stones.

Found wild in the forests of Japan and eastern China is the Japanese cedar, *Cryptomeria japonica,* an evergreen tree with spiky leaves and knobbly cones. It can survive to a great age, 7,000 years is the latest scientific estimate. Japanese cedars are planted to form scenic avenues or grown in plantations to yield a strong, durable, red-brown timber. Also grown in groves, but for its leaves rather than its wood, is the mulberry, a deciduous tree native to China. The heart-shaped leaves are the food of the silkworm caterpillar, and mulberry trees play an important part in the natural silk industry.

Japan is the home of the wild chrysanthemum, a perennial plant with daisy-shaped flowers that spring on woody stalks from a strong rootstock. Under cultivation it has produced a wealth of decorative forms in a full range of colours.

The Himalayan foothills have a cold temperate climate because, although situated in the tropics, they stand many thousands of feet above sea level. Winters are snowy, and cold springs and hot summers are followed by heavy, warm autumn monsoon rains. Evergreen forests prevail, with the stately Himalayan cedar, or deodar, prominent among the conifers. Its strong, naturally durable and fragrant timber is used for building, furniture, railway ties, or sleepers, and telegraph poles. Leathery-leaved, evergreen rhododendrons form thickets beneath the cedars. On the forest floor the warmth of late spring calls into growth the perennial primulas, which store food in fleshy rootstocks. Their rosettes of leaves hold central stalks that carry the flower-heads. A common variety is the drumstick primula, *Primula denticulata,* often grown in western gardens.

Right: an Indian girl gathers tea from bushes grown beneath shade trees. The regular picking of leaves and shoots maintains the bushes' even shape.

The most economic crop on these slopes is the native tea plant, an evergreen bush that can grow, on fertile ground, the whole year round. As each fresh flush of leaves and buds appears, which can be every seven or eight days during the autumn monsoon rains, it is plucked by nimble-fingered girls. This foliage is fermented at the estate factory, dried, and exported to all parts of the world. The refreshing drink made by pouring boiling water on the leaves contains a stimulating alkaloid called theine, or caffeine.

North of the Himalayas a huge expanse of low-rainfall country, with freezing winters and hot, dry summers, stretches from the Ural Mountains eastward across Asia to the China seas. The effective growing season here is so short that only pasture grasses, needing little moisture, can thrive. These support the flocks and animal herds of nomadic peoples.

One of the plants that survives on these Asian steppes is wild rhubarb. It is left untouched by animals because its fleshy green leaves are rich in a poisonous salt that makes them unpalatable. The fleshy red stalks that shoot up each spring from the bulbous rootstock are perfectly edible when cooked. In cultivation these stalks are often forced with heat in darkened houses, to keep them tender. When flowering, rhubarb plants send up tall stalks bearing many feather white blossoms.

Hemp, also native to northern Asia, is a tall annual with deeply divided leaves. It yields a strong fibre used for ropes and nets, which is obtained by beating and washing the stems. Hemp is the source of the drug cannabis, also called "pot," *dagga, marijuana,* and *hashish,* which is so dangerous that many countries ban hemp cultivation altogether. The round, oily seeds are harmless, however, and are often used to feed birds.

To the north of the grassy steppes lies a zone in which, although rainfall is scanty, little moisture evaporates because the temperature remains low. Here lies the taiga, a continuous stretch of coniferous forest, mainly of spruces, running from Finland eastward to the Bering Strait. Birch, juniper, willow, and alder grow there too, along with pine and larch. The slow-growing, evergreen spruces cast a deep shade, excluding lesser plants. Their timber, exported as "whitewood," is excellent for building, joinery, and paper pulp, but transport is difficult since most of the great rivers run north to the Arctic Ocean, which is frozen for most of the year.

Still closer to the northern edge of the continent, where it borders the Arctic Ocean, is the tundra, a zone where low plants strive to grow on permafrost—a peaty soil frozen solid all winter through. In summer the upper layers thaw, but a few feet down the frost persists. Only shallow-rooted, short-season plants can exist. One is the dryas, which forms perennial tufts of woody stems and opens dark-green leaves, silvery below, in May. Its white, eight-petalled blossoms follow, to be succeeded in August by large, feathery seed-heads.

Another tundra plant is the dwarf willow which, in late spring, sends woody stems creeping through the undergrowth,

Hemp (top left) is grown for tough rope fibres. Rhubarb (centre) is a wild plant long cultivated for its tasty, succulent red stems. Dwarf willow (bottom left) forms a creeping tundra shrub; note male catkins.

bearing either male or female catkins, according to the sex of each plant. When drainage is impeded, sphagnum moss builds up its soft, water-drenched mats. As the tips of the stems grow upwards the bases decay, forming brown peat that can eventually become many feet thick.

All these tundra plants are flexible, able to survive the repeated movements of soils that rise when they freeze in autumn, and fall with the spring thaw. All are low, since taller plants could not remain upright under the harsh conditions. They give man no shelter from the bitter winds that sweep across these barren wastes from the polar ice-fields to the north.

Sphagnum moss (centre right) grows in dense tufts on tundra peat bogs. Dryas (bottom centre) has long trailing stems that survive soil changes due to freezing and thawing. South of the tundra, spruce trees (right) form vast evergreen forests, valued for timber; they bear drooping brown cones.

4
Africa

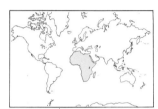

Tropical timber forests of West Africa. Savannas and Saharan desert fringes, with date palms and millet cultivation. South Africa's gaily flowering aloes and gladioli. Desert plants that mimic stones.

Africa is the only continent to stretch for equal distances north and south of the equator, and to show similar zones of plant life on either side. The yearly swing of the sun, from the Tropic of Cancer in the north to the Tropic of Capricorn in the south, is reflected in the march of Africa's seasons. Between November and April, when the sun is highest there, the seasonal rains fall south of the equator, leaving the north-central regions, such as the Sudan, hot and dry. From May to October more rain falls in the north, again under the highest phase of the sun, while southern Africa in its turn suffers drought under cloudless skies. Only the equatorial belt along the Gulf of Guinea and in the Congo Basin enjoys year-round high temperatures and high rainfall to support its tall rain forests.

Most of the continent of Africa is a high plateau tilted down towards the north; on all the other sides great rivers make sharp descents by rapids or waterfalls to narrow coastal plains. This high elevation keeps the climate cooler than elsewhere in the tropics and favours settlement and the cultivation of temperate-zone crops.

Under the constant heat, rainfall, and high humidity of the Guinea coast, tall forest trees grow quickly to great size. A typical one is the sapele, also called African mahogany, which has an immense, smooth-barked trunk up to 150 feet tall and 20 feet round. Its base is supported by plank-shaped buttresses, which oblige tree-fellers to work from platforms set 10 feet or so above the ground, where the trunk becomes narrower. High in its crown the sapele bears thick, evergreen, compound leaves, clusters of yellow flowers, and oval pods holding many large, hard seeds. Its timber, which shows the attractive pattern of alternating red and pink stripes, is hard and strong.

Ebony, a smaller tree, also grows in the rain forest, in the shade of taller forest giants. It has been valued since ancient times for its jet-black, lustrous heartwood. Ebony has a round

Tropical rain forest in Central Africa. Sapele (right), a giant timber tree, rises from a buttressed base. Lesser trees are oil palm (centre) and ebony (fallen log). On the jungle floor grow white arum lilies, African violets, strelitzias with pointed flower-heads, and sansevieria with variegated leaves (left). White stephanotis climbs a tree trunk (right).

trunk, with squarish plates of rugged bark, leathery, oval leaves, solitary white, star-shaped flowers, and small, round fruits set on short stalks. The hard, smooth timber is used in decorative woodwork, particularly as a black inlay amid woods of other colours, and for musical instruments, such as flutes.

Many palms thrive in these rain forests and one, the African oil palm, yields a valuable edible oil that now features largely in world trade. A short, stumpy tree when young, it bears a crown of huge, feather-shaped, compound leaves, with glossy, dark-green leaflets. Amidst these the flower spikes spring up, all the year round, some bearing loose clusters of yellow male flowers and others dense groups of brown female ones. The latter ripen quickly, forming bunches of brown fruits, each holding a hard, brown seed within a layer of thick, oily, yellow pulp. This nutritious pulp can be eaten raw, or processed to extract the oil, which is used either in cookery or to make soap or margarine.

On the forest floor, in clearings, and along its fringes, grow many decorative plants, some of which are cultivated in green-houses or as house plants in temperate lands. One of the most striking is the strelitzia, or bird-of-paradise flower, a sturdy plant with sword-shaped leaves, which bears a flower-head shaped like the head and sharply-pointed beak of a bird. This is green in colour, and bears a cluster of yellow and blue petals close to its base. These attract small nectar-seeking birds to the flower, which is more often pollinated by the feet of honey-

Cultivated food plants of moist tropical Africa. The water melon (above left) is grown as a climber, holding itself up by twisting tendrils on upright poles. The pod below its small, bright flower ripens quickly to the large luscious fruit, which holds many edible seeds within its soft pulp. Okra (above) is a tall annual plant with spreading foliage and handsome yellow flowers like hollyhocks. Its narrow seed-pods are cooked as vegetables.

The yam, a staple food of many West African communities, is the underground storage root of a slender climber. Yam stems need upright supports to expand their heart-shaped leaves. When fully grown, the yams are dug up and stored in racks, exposed to the air, until needed.

birds than by insects. Concealed in the dim jungle shades, and also found in wet grassy stretches on more open land, the white arum lily bears a conspicuous and beautiful white spathe that encircles the true flower spike. This spathe attracts insects to the plant. They alight on the strongly-scented, club-shaped stem within it and crawl down this to its foot, where they brush past a group of bristles which trap them within a circular chamber. Once the female flowers there have been fertilized by pollen brought from another lily, the bristles wither and the insects escape, to carry pollen to another flower.

Many plants found in these tropical jungles have no resting period, growing steadily the whole year round. The sansevieria, often grown in one of its variegated forms as a decorative plant, follows this pattern. As well as bearing seeds, it spreads by means of natural offshoots that spring from its tuberous root-stock. The lovely African violets, or saintpaulias, thrive throughout the year on the thick mat of leaf-mould and rotting twigs that forms on the forest floor. They grow in conditions of constant heat, deep shade, and a continually moist atmosphere. Their thick, oval, dark-green leaves are borne on stout stalks that spring straight from ground level. Delicate sprays of deep violet-blue flowers arise on slender stems from the same leaf-stalk rosette.

In Madagascar the exquisite stephanotis grows as a vigorous evergreen climber in the moist air of the shady rain forest. It bears pale-green oval leaves, thick in texture, with a waxy surface. The fragrant white flowers, carried abundantly in long sprays, look as though each has been carved from ivory.

Since there are no clearly marked seasons in the wet tropical zone, cultivators prefer to raise food crops that mature the whole year round. The yam, *Dioscorea rotundata*, a staple food in West Africa, is raised by placing the crown of a tuber in the ground and training the shoots, which spring from its buds, up long stakes. After a growing spell of some eight to twelve months, the large, brown tuber that has matured below ground is harvested. Yams are rich in starch, but hold little protein. They can be stored for months by hanging them on strings exposed to the air, under cover to keep them dry.

Another widely cultivated climber is the water melon, which is grown from seed on damp rich soil. It sends up quickly-growing stems that bear tendrils to grasp supports, and opens small, yellow flowers. The fruit, which ripens rapidly, is black and dark-green, globe-shaped or oval, and up to one foot across.

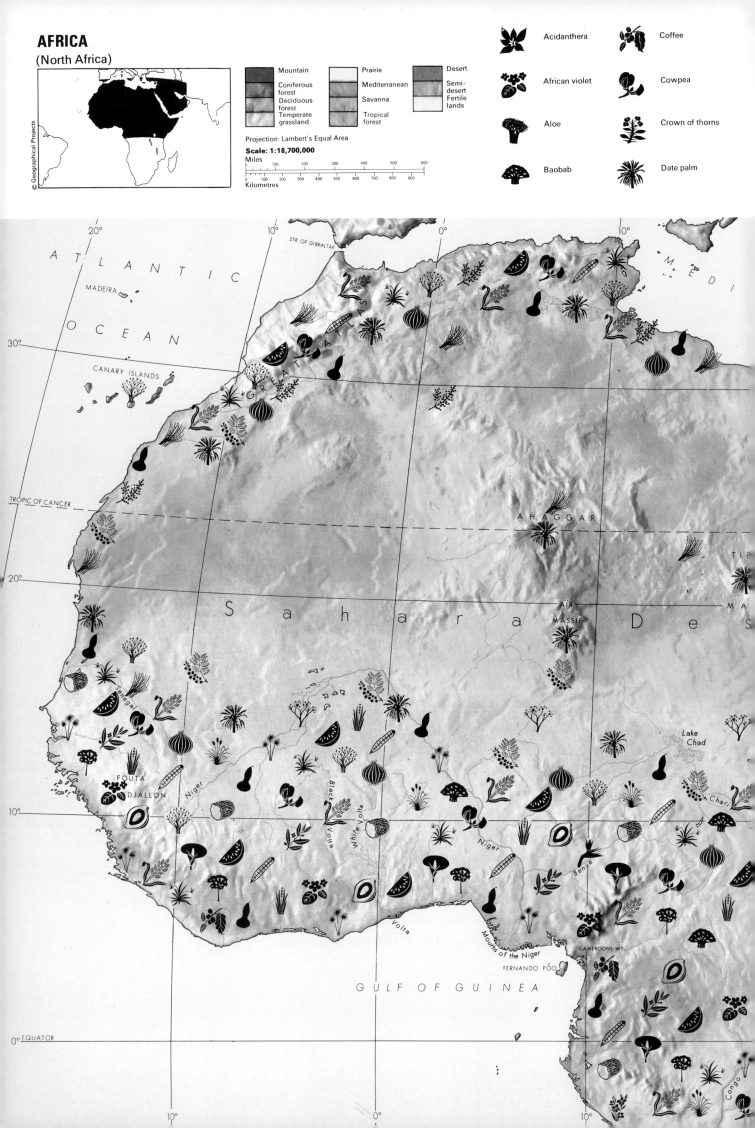

AFRICA
(North Africa)

© Geographical Projects

Mountain
Coniferous forest
Deciduous forest
Temperate grassland

Prairie
Mediterranean
Savanna
Tropical forest

Desert
Semi-desert
Fertile lands

Projection: Lambert's Equal Area

Scale: 1:18,700,000

Miles
Kilometres

Acidanthera

African violet

Aloe

Baobab

Coffee

Cowpea

Crown of thorns

Date palm

ATLANTIC

OCEAN

MADEIRA

CANARY ISLANDS

TROPIC OF CANCER

STR. OF GIBRALTAR

MEDI

GREAT ATLAS

AHAGGAR

AÏR MASSIF

TIB

MA

Sahara Des

Senegal

Niger

FOUTA DJALLON

Black Volta

White Volta

Niger

Benue

Volta

Mouths of the Niger

CAMEROONS MT.

FERNANDO PÓO

Lake Chad

Chari

GULF OF GUINEA

Congo

EQUATOR

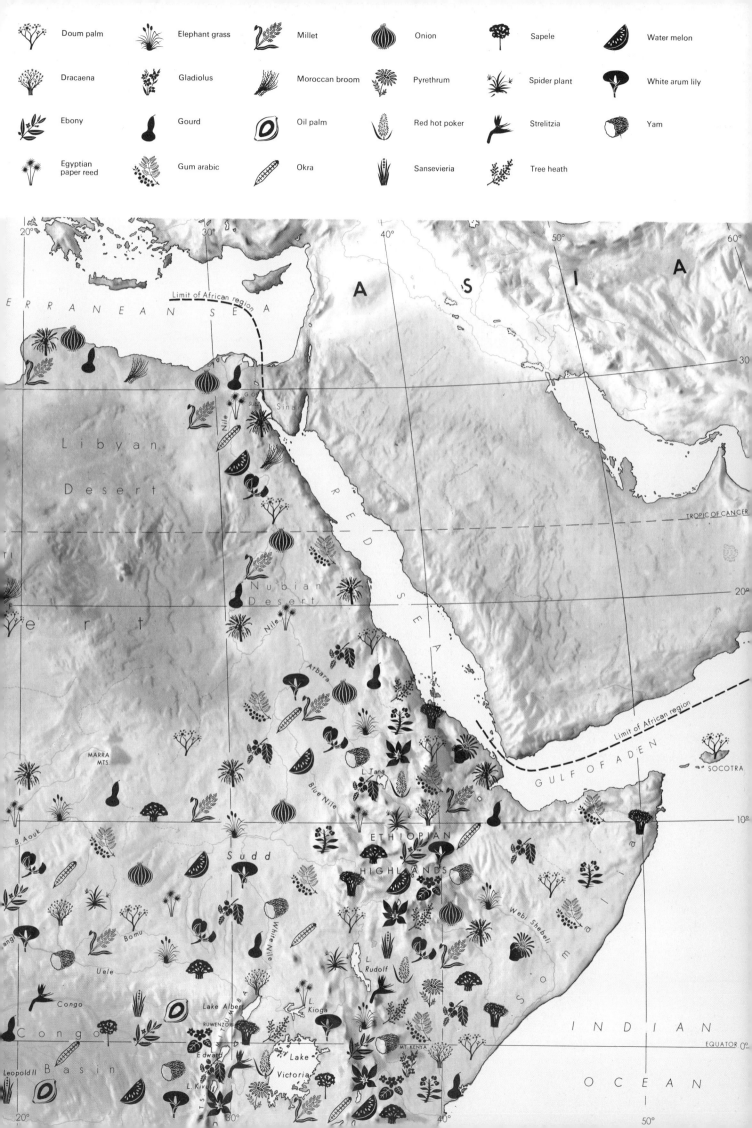

Doum palm	Elephant grass	Millet	Onion	Sapele	Water melon
Dracaena	Gladiolus	Moroccan broom	Pyrethrum	Spider plant	White arum lily
Ebony	Gourd	Oil palm	Red hot poker	Strelitzia	Yam
Egyptian paper reed	Gum arabic	Okra	Sansevieria	Tree heath	

It holds sweet and juicy flesh that may be white, yellow, or red in colour. Embedded in this are many flat seeds which may be white, brown, or black. They are oily and nutritious, and are often eaten as a delicacy.

Okra, also called gumbo, is a very popular green vegetable in tropical Africa, and is now grown in most warm lands. The bushy plant, easily raised from seed, carries broad, deeply lobed leaves and yellow flowers, like those of the garden hibiscus. Its seed-pods, which are gathered and eaten while still green and unripe, hold a soft mucilage with a pleasing flavour.

The African savannas, dry grasslands with scattered trees, extend in an enormous arc to the north, east, and south of the tropical rain forests. Their seasonal rainfall supports perennial grasses, including the elephant grass, which puts down deep roots to help it survive droughts. During the rainy season it sends up slender leaf blades and feathery flower spikes, both over six feet high.

The characteristic tree of this region is the baobab, easily known by its huge, swollen trunk containing soft tissue that stores water through the dry season. Though seldom over 70 feet tall it often exceeds 60 feet in girth. The slender branches that emerge from the trunk look like roots, and hence the baobab is sometimes called the "upside-down-tree." The

fibrous bark is used by the Africans to make fish nets, ropes, sacks, and rough clothing. The baobab bears large, compound leaves with three to five leaflets spreading out like fingers of a hand, each five inches long. Its large, drooping, fragrant flowers have five recurved petals and a projecting group of purple stamens. The huge, sausage-shaped fruits hold about 30 seeds within a mass of mealy, acid pulp. Both seeds and flesh are eaten by monkeys and also by wandering hunting tribesmen who regard them as a staple food.

On the drier, semi-desert grasslands of the Sudan the quaint doum palm is the typical tree. Distinguished from most other palms by the way in which its trunk divides into several branches, the doum palm can survive desert conditions provided its roots tap ground water. Its edible and nutritious soft fruits hold white seeds so hard that they are often called "vegetable ivory." They are carved into buttons, needles, and ornaments. In the western semi-deserts the dracaenas, tree-like plants which have a growth habit similar to that of the doum palm, flourish under equally dry conditions. Related to the lilies, they bear sword-shaped leaves in tufts at the tips of their branches and large spikes of white blossoms.

Most savanna shrubs are strongly armed with sharp spines to check the browsing animals that would otherwise destroy them. They include spiny euphorbias such as the "crown of thorns,"

Remarkable East African dry-country plants, often cultivated in greenhouses and tropical gardens, are shown below. The spider plant (overlapping baobab) spreads by natural layers. The crown of thorns, armed with fierce spines to check browsing animals, bears vivid red flowers. At bottom right is the acidanthera, a bulbous plant with nodding blossoms shaped like butterflies.

AFFRICA
(South Africa)

© Geographical Projects

Mountain
Coniferous forest
Deciduous forest
Temperate grassland
Mediterranean
Savanna
Tropical forest
Desert
Semi-desert

Projection: Lambert's Equal Area

Scale: 1:18,700,000

Miles
0   100   200   300   400   500   600

Kilometres
0   100   200   300   400   500   600   700   800   900

Acidanthera		Millet
African violet		Oil palm
Aloe		Okra
Baobáb		Onion
Clivia		Pelargonium
Coffee		Pyrethrum
Cowpea		Red hot poker
Crown of thorns		Sansevieria
Date palm		Sapele
Doum palm		Spider plant
Dracaena		Stephanotis
Ebony		Stone plant
Egyptian paper reed		Strelitzia
Elephant grass		Tree heath
Gladiolus		Water melon
Gourd		Welwitschia
Gum arabic		White arum lily
Mesembry-anthemum		Yam

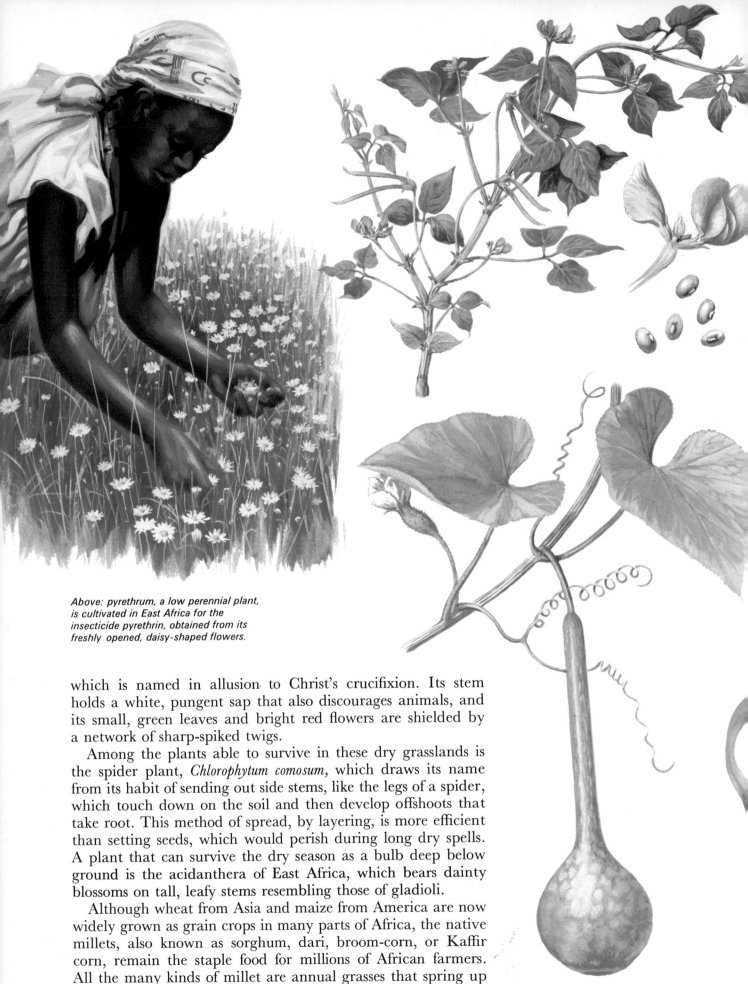

Above: pyrethrum, a low perennial plant, is cultivated in East Africa for the insecticide pyrethrin, obtained from its freshly opened, daisy-shaped flowers.

Cowpea (centre top) is one of many climbers grown for protein-rich seeds. Gourds (above), also borne by climbing plants, serve as fruits or storage vessels.

which is named in allusion to Christ's crucifixion. Its stem holds a white, pungent sap that also discourages animals, and its small, green leaves and bright red flowers are shielded by a network of sharp-spiked twigs.

Among the plants able to survive in these dry grasslands is the spider plant, *Chlorophytum comosum*, which draws its name from its habit of sending out side stems, like the legs of a spider, which touch down on the soil and then develop offshoots that take root. This method of spread, by layering, is more efficient than setting seeds, which would perish during long dry spells. A plant that can survive the dry season as a bulb deep below ground is the acidanthera of East Africa, which bears dainty blossoms on tall, leafy stems resembling those of gladioli.

Although wheat from Asia and maize from America are now widely grown as grain crops in many parts of Africa, the native millets, also known as sorghum, dari, broom-corn, or Kaffir corn, remain the staple food for millions of African farmers. All the many kinds of millet are annual grasses that spring up rapidly from seed sown on cultivated soil just before the rains begin, and ripen heads of grain during the dry season. The individual seeds are small, round, and hard. They vary in colour

Left: millet, Africa's native cereal, ripens multitudes of small hard seeds in feathery clusters.

from white to yellow and brown, and may be borne in close spikes or in loose open panicles. All are apt to fall or "shatter" as soon as they are ripe, and therefore the crop must be promptly harvested, threshed, and stored. Millets are made into coarse bread, or cooked like porridge. If fermented, they yield an alcoholic drink resembling beer.

Many leguminous plants are grown throughout Africa because of their pleasant flavours and their nutritious proteins. The cowpea, a typical native kind, is grown as an annual climbing plant, particularly in the high rainfall region of West Africa. After only two months growth, its green pods can be picked for eating as a vegetable. If left, they mature as very long, pinkish-brown, slender, papery pods, holding many small, hard, pink seeds, which can be stored dry for eating later.

Many kinds of gourds are grown to provide either a pleasantly flavoured green vegetable, or handy pots and storage vessels. All are trailing plants with divided, hairy leaves and bright, usually yellow, flowers. The seed-pods at the base of each flower swell rapidly to form large, soft fruits of various shapes, which are gathered when still green for cooking and eating. If allowed to ripen, many kinds develop a hard, brown, woody skin, and when the flesh and seeds have been scooped out of this, the gourd makes a good container for liquids or food-stuffs. Gourds are also made into musical instruments, including rattles, and are carved and painted as ornaments.

In East Africa many farmers grow pyrethrum, a low plant with daisy-shaped flowers that hold a natural insecticide. These blossoms are harvested soon after they open and are processed to obtain pyrethrin, the active constituent. Pyrethrin has the unusual property called "knock-down," which means that it paralyzes the insect instantaneously, allowing stronger chemicals in the insecticide to complete the kill.

Though most of northern Africa is desert or nearly so, the various ranges of the Atlas and Ahaggar mountains, the Tibesti Massif and the highlands of Ethiopia have enough seasonal rain to support drought-resistant plants. The Moroccan broom, so called because its bunches of twigs can be used for sweeping dust, is a typical "switch" plant. It has dense clusters of fine, green twigs which do most of the work of photosynthesis, and cause little water-loss. Its leaves, which would lose more water if they developed, remain small. Moroccan broom bears masses of bright orange flowers, shaped like sweet peas. These mature to form papery pods, holding hard seeds.

Around the Mediterranean shores the white tree heath grows as a tall shrub with a woody stem, stout enough to form the timber used for making briar smoking pipes. The tiny leaves of all heaths are crowded close on tough twigs, and are curved inwardly on each other to resist water-loss. The white tree heath, which forms dense thickets, is smothered in mauvish-white, bell-shaped blossoms every spring.

Wherever water is found, along the few rivers and in the oases, the date palm is cultivated as a source of nourishing and delicious fruit. It forms a sturdy, long-lived tree with several stems springing from its root base, each bearing a tuft of huge, feathery, compound leaves at its summit. Each tree is either male or female. Arab growers plant only enough males to ensure the pollination needed to secure fruit. Male flowers, which consist of long strands of yellow anthers, are often hung amid the flower-spikes of female trees for this purpose. Female flowers grow in large, feathery clusters, which mature as huge bunches of yellowish-brown dates. Within a tough skin, each date has soft, sweet, yellow flesh, rich in sugar and vitamins, surrounding a long, hard, greyish-brown seed. The softer, sweeter dates are eaten as they ripen; the harder kinds can be stored and form a staple food for many desert peoples.

A plant adapted to life in arid lands and which is cultivated in the semi-desert areas of northern Africa is the onion. Each onion arises from a seed that sprouts in wet weather and grows into a sturdy plant with long, narrow, fleshy, and drought-resistant leaves. As cold, or dry, weather approaches, the onion stores food in its bulb, which is made up of white, swollen scale leaves, surrounded by a brown, papery skin to check water-loss. Hence, it is easily stored, and at this stage most onions are harvested for food. If allowed to grow on, the onion uses up the food reserves from its bulb to produce a huge, round flower-head, made up of scores of small, star-shaped purple blossoms that eventually shed myriads of black seeds.

A quaint plant of north African rivers, lakes, and marshes is the Egyptian paper reed, also called papyrus, a tall aquatic grass with stiff, green stems up to 10 feet tall. These carry, clear of the water in which the reed grows, large tufts of slender leaves, spreading out like plumes of feathers. Small, green flower-spikes appear amid these leaf clusters. The ancient Egyptians often featured this reed in their art forms and also made the world's first paper from its stems.

Coffee, now widely grown in India, Arabia, the West Indies, and Brazil, originated in north-east Africa. It is a small, sturdy tree with dark-green, oval leaves, always set in pairs, which have a waxy surface and thick texture to check the loss of water during droughts. White, star-shaped, fragrant flowers open in dense clusters at leaf axils along its twigs. After pollination they develop into bunches of fleshy, red berries, each holding soft pulp and two hard seeds—the coffee beans. After harvesting, the pulp is removed by hand or machine to expose the beans, which at this stage are still in their pale-green "parchment" skin. This is later removed to obtain the familiar greyish-brown, flat-sided, oval bean, which is roasted and ground.

The fringes of Africa's northern deserts, from Senegal east to Somaliland, and many dry savannas farther south, are the home of many kinds of acacia, or thorn tree. As the name suggests, all bear sharp thorns to protect their twigs from browsing beasts, though in fact many antelopes, giraffes, camels, and even domestic farm stock eat their leaves and seed-pods, thorns and all. Their roots, which range widely and deeply into the soil in search of scarce moisture, bear nodules which fix nitrogen. African acacias have finely-divided leaves, and masses of yellow flowers, which look like powder-puffs because of their

North African shrubs, plants, and trees. Gum arabic and stem gum (top left). Coffee (above) with soft fruits holding berries. Egyptian paper reed (centre). Date palm with fruit clusters (top right). Onions (far right).

Shrubs that defy drought in north-west Africa. Above: tree heath, with narrow, clustered leaves. Right: Moroccan broom bears stems that act as leaves.

numerous golden stamens. Thorn trees often assume odd, flat-topped umbrella shapes, spreading sideways above the level to which hungry animals can reach. *Acacia senegal* and related species are the source of gum arabic. Nomadic Arabs in Somaliland and the Sudan tap the trees by stripping off patches of bark, returning to collect the sticky substance that oozes out and dries to a firm, white mass in the desert air. Gum arabic is used in adhesives, polishes, inks, pottery pigments, textile finishing, and as a glaze for confectionery and in pharmacy.

South Africa is the homeland of many fine decorative plants that developed in isolation from other floras, but have now been introduced to most tropical and many temperate-climate lands. The most widely grown are the pelargoniums, also called geraniums. They are tough and rather woody perennial plants with hairy leaves that help them resist drought. The whole plant is pervaded by the strongly fragrant oil of geranium, widely used in perfumery. They carry bold masses of flowers, which are borne clear of the foliage.

The aptly named red hot poker, a hardier South African plant, forms clumps of tough, narrow, pointed greyish-green leaves, often three feet long. From the heart of each clump the tall flower spikes arise, late in summer, to heights of six feet or more. At the tip of each round, pointed flower-head the numerous tube-shaped flowers, which point downwards, are at

On the South African veldt, tall aloes,
like this kokkerboom tree, raise tufts
of waxy foliage on much-divided stems.

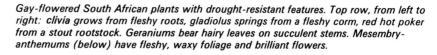

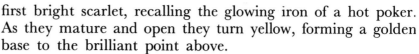

Gay-flowered South African plants with drought-resistant features. Top row, from left to right: clivia grows from fleshy roots, gladiolus springs from a fleshy corm, red hot poker from a stout rootstock. Geraniums bear hairy leaves on succulent stems. Mesembry-anthemums (below) have fleshy, waxy foliage and brilliant flowers.

first bright scarlet, recalling the glowing iron of a hot poker. As they mature and open they turn yellow, forming a golden base to the brilliant point above.

The clivia, or Kaffir lily, is a beautiful South African perennial that can be grown in northern lands only as an indoor plant. It has a large underground rootstock and perennial, dark-green, strap-shaped leaves in two ranks, up to two inches wide by two feet long. The whole structure is well suited to retain water. The clivia's flower stalk carries a spreading cluster of handsome orange-red, trumpet-shaped blossoms with golden centres, which are eventually succeeded by red berries.

Several sorts of gladioli, which grow wild in South Africa, have been developed into horticultural varieties. In temperate countries the growers substitute a cold season resting period for the natural dry season one. Gladioli pass this resting time as firm round corms, protected against drying out by papery, pinkish-brown skins. When growth begins, each corm sends up a shoot that carries sword-shaped, pale-green leaves; the Latin name *gladiolus* signifies "a little sword." The flower spike that springs from these leaves is often four feet tall and carries a succession of trumpet-shaped blossoms that, in modern cultivated kinds, may be of any conceivable colour; the wild common kind has crimson blooms.

In the deserts and along the seashores of the Cape grow a great variety of fleshy succulents designed, like cacti, to stand arid conditions. Among them are many kinds of mesembry-anthemum, a name meaning "mid-day flower," because they open their daisy-shaped blossoms around noon. They have bluish-green, cylindrical, fleshy stems and leaves, which together hold their water reserves. One common kind, called the Hottentot fig, has pink-and-white flowers and a juicy, edible fruit. In certain species the seed capsules remain tightly closed until soaked by water, which ensures that seeds cannot escape and start growth until moisture is present for their survival.

Under even drier conditions grow the stone plants, which resemble pebbles and so usually escape being eaten by hungry animals. Each "living stone" consists of two swollen, fleshy, mottled leaves on a rudimentary stem rooted in the arid soil. Eventually it bears, between these leaves, a brightly-coloured, daisy-shaped flower that is almost as large as the rest of the plant.

In the torrid deserts of south-west Africa grows the miracle plant, *Welwitschia mirabilis*. A "living fossil," it is unlike all other plants and has no surviving near relations. Each individual welwitschia plant consists of two huge leaves, growing flat over the sand, in opposite directions, from a low, stout, woody stem. As these leaves, sometimes 10 feet long and 4 feet wide, become tattered and withered at their tips, they are renewed by fresh growth at their bases, and this structure may persist for 1,000 years or more. Each welwitschia is either male or female; both sexes bear stalked, ovoid spikes of primitive flowers, which are wind-pollinated. The seeds bear wings and are dispersed by the winds that sweep across the hot desert sands. Most miracle plants grow near the Atlantic seacoast, and gain water from sea fogs driven inland by the wind.

Left: plants of the arid southern African desert. Welwitschia (far left) spreads two leaves from a stem edged with flowers. Stone plants (left) resemble pebbles.

5 North America

Canadian sprucewoods, cotton-grass swamps and tundras. Forests of maple, oak, and beech in the eastern United States. California's mammoth redwoods. Sub-tropical plants of Mexico and the Caribbean.

North America forms a great triangle with the base in the north. There, the snowy tundras of Alaska, Canada, and Greenland, with bitterly cold winters but long sunlit summer days, stretch for 4,000 miles, nearly halfway around the globe. To the south, the continent steadily narrows until it merges into the Isthmus of Panama linking it with South America. Here it runs deep into the tropics. The warm Pacific and Atlantic Oceans, together with the Caribbean Sea and the Gulf of Mexico, maintain the heat and moisture. In the south-east, Cuba, Jamaica, and the lesser islands of the Caribbean Sea enjoy a remarkably equable sub-tropical climate.

The north and east of Canada form a vast level plain studded with lakes and threaded by slow winding rivers that are ice-bound throughout the long winter. Plant life is markedly seasonal. Broad-leaved trees, adapted to make good use of sunlight during long summer days, flourish where warmth and moisture are adequate. The sugar maple illustrates this annual growth rhythm in a striking way. When the thaw comes in spring, the sugar maple mobilizes the food reserves stored in its living wood cells as a strong current of sap, flowing upwards, to nourish its bursting shoots and leaf buds. Farmers tap their "sugar bushes" by boring a hole in each tree and directing the sap-flow through a spout into a cup, They concentrate the sweet juice, on the same day, into maple syrup or tasty maple candy. During the bright summer the maples renew their food reserves, flower and ripen winged seeds. Then, in the autumn, their leaves change to brilliant shades of orange and red before drifting to the woodland floor.

Trees that range farther north include the birches with their silver bark, long used by the Indians to make birch-bark canoes, and the streamside aspen poplars. Aspen leaves tremble incessantly on long slender stalks, under the slightest breath of

Autumn beside a lake in eastern Canada, when leaves of paper birches (right) and aspen poplars (left) become brilliant gold. Maples (seen distantly) flame bright orange. On swampy muskeg shrubby juniper and creeping cranberry (both inset) ripen soft fruits among white seed-heads of cotton grass. Inset, left: yellow water lily.

wind. This aids air circulation through their leaves, and assists nutrition by supplying more carbon dioxide for photosynthesis, though it makes for rapid water-loss.

On the surface of still, open lakes, shallow ponds, and sluggish streams the yellow water lily, also called the bullhead lily, opens its glossy, dark-green heart-shaped leaves. Its large floating flowers are ball-shaped, composed of many incurved golden sepals, holding within them smaller petals, yellow stamens, and a round disc-shaped, cream-coloured stigma.

Forests of evergreen conifers, often intermixed with broad-leaved trees, extend across northern Canada. Owing to the brief summers, their growth is slow, but they form a vast reserve of softwood timber for sawmills and paper-mills. Three closely allied spruces—the white, the red, and the black—are the most useful of the softwoods. Farther north, the almost worthless jack pine forms low open scrub.

Junipers grow as low bushes, able to resist both bitter freezing winds and deep winter snow. The sharp points of their leaves, which hold a pungent resin, protect them from grazing animals.

Common trees of New England woods. Flame-shaped leaves of red oak (top left) turn crimson in autumn. Hemlock (left of centre) is a graceful evergreen with drooping branches and brown cones. Persimmon (centre) seen here in leafless winter outline, bears soft orange fruits. Evening primrose (above) is a frequent, though short-lived, plant of woodland fringes and wasteland.

In autumn they bear purple berries, which attract the birds that spread their small hard seeds.

In the swamps the cotton grass raises its brown, wiry stalks, topped in midsummer by white seed-heads. It is one of many low, peat-forming plants able to live on soil frozen for half the year and sodden for most of the short summer. Under these conditions the faded stems and dead roots scarcely decay at all, so that the bed of peat grows steadily deeper, with just a thin layer of living plants clothing the surface. Through this zone creeps the cranberry, its wiry, perennial stems resistant to movement of the peat caused by freezing, thawing, or flooding. In midsummer it opens pink, bell-shaped flowers, followed in autumn by delicious red berries.

Farther north still, on the barren tundra, where a few feet below the surface the soil remains permanently frozen, primitive lichens take the place of higher plants. Each lichen "plant" consists of a green alga united to a grey fungus. One of the largest is reindeer "moss," which forms the main food for roving herds of caribou.

Despite its hard, snowy winters, the north-eastern United States has a warm summer climate. Ample, well-distributed rainfall is induced by the hill ranges when the prevailing south-westerly winds blow in from the Gulf of Mexico. This coastal region provided a favourable setting for the settlements of the early colonists, who were able to cultivate the same crops, and to carry on the same farm husbandry, as they had known in Europe. But although the name "New England" fits it well, there are many native trees and flowers that have no counterparts in western Europe.

The north-east's most distinctive broad-leaved trees are the red oaks, of which there are several local species. All alike have sharply lobed, flame-shaped leaves which, in summer, reveal crimson overtones to their prevailing dark green. In autumn they change to brilliant red and orange shades before they fall. The timber of these bright-foliaged trees lacks the great strength and durability of the American white oak, but it is a good general-purpose hardwood, suitable for furniture and making paper, or as fuel.

A common evergreen conifer of this region, the hemlock, was

Every spring the shrubby flowering dogwood (top right) displays gay clusters of blossoms. In early summer the nodding flowers of Canada lily (centre) open in pairs, down near the forest floor. Here too is found showy lady's slipper orchid (above). In autumn the highbush blueberry (top, right of centre), which contrasts with creeping kinds, bears fruits on shrubby stems.

71

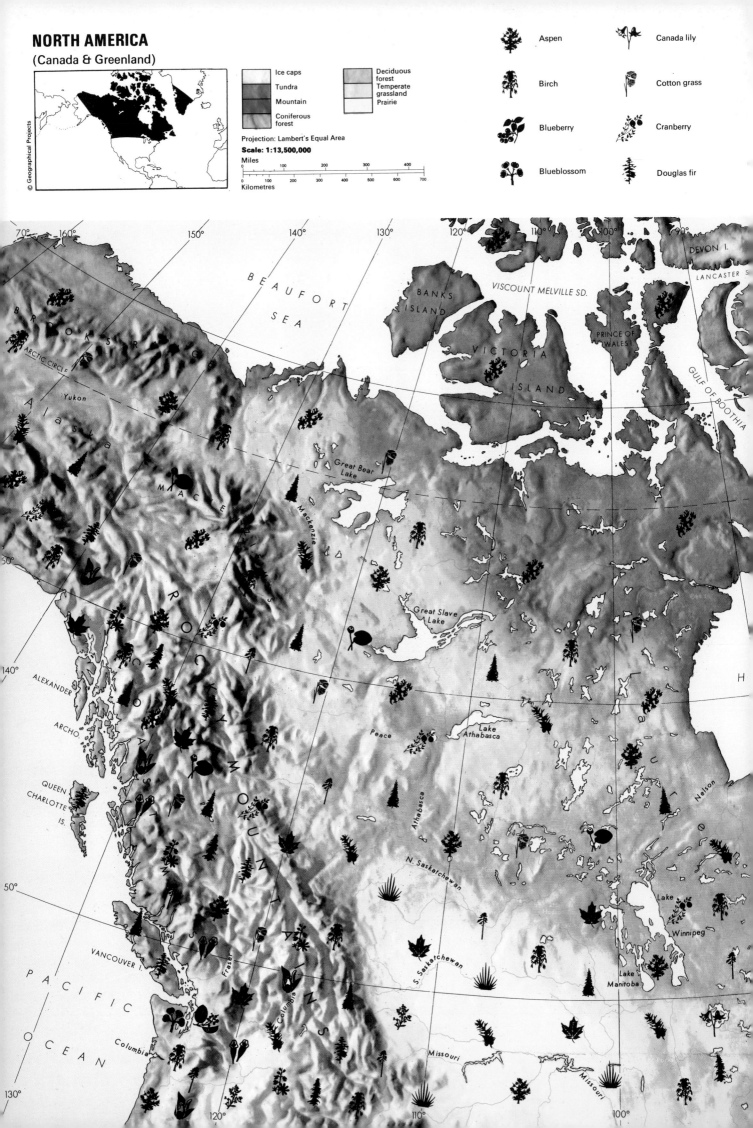

NORTH AMERICA
(Canada & Greenland)

© Geographical Projects

Ice caps		Deciduous forest	
Tundra		Temperate grassland	
Mountain		Prairie	
Coniferous forest			

Projection: Lambert's Equal Area

Scale: 1:13,500,000

Miles
0   100   200   300   400

Kilometres
0 100 200 300 400 500 600 700

Aspen
Birch
Blueberry
Blueblossom

Canada lily
Cotton grass
Cranberry
Douglas fir

BEAUFORT SEA

BANKS ISLAND

VISCOUNT MELVILLE SD.

DEVON I.

LANCASTER S.

VICTORIA ISLAND

PRINCE OF WALES I.

GULF OF BOOTHIA

B R O O K S   R G E

ARCTIC CIRCLE

Yukon

Alaska

M A C K E

Great Bear Lake

Mackenzie

Great Slave Lake

R O C K Y

Peace

Lake Athabasca

ALEXANDER

ARCHO.

Athabasca

QUEEN CHARLOTTE IS.

M O U N T A I N S

N. Saskatchewan

Nelson

Lake Winnipeg

50°

S. Saskatchewan

Lake Manitoba

VANCOUVER I.

Fraser

Columbia

PACIFIC OCEAN

Columbia

Missouri

Missouri

130°

120°

110°

100°

Evening primrose

Flowering dogwood

Hemlock

Juniper

Madrone

Maple

Pasture grass

Pine

Pitcher plant (Sarracenia)

Red oak

Reindeer mos

Sagebrush

Skunk cabbage

Snakemouth flower

Spruce

Wild lupin

Yellow water lily

70°   60°   50°   40°   70°   30°   ARCTIC CIRCLE

G R E E N L A N D

60°

BAFFIN BAY

40°

B A F F I N   I S L A N D

DAVIS STRAIT

FOXE BASIN

SOUTHAMPTON ISLAND

HUDSON STRAIT

A T L A N T I C   O C E A N

H U D S O N   B A Y

Ungava Peninsula

L a b r a d o r

50°

50°

NEWFOUNDLAND

JAMES BAY

Severn

Lake Mistassini

ANTICOSTI I.

GULF OF ST. LAWRENCE

S h i e l d

L A U R E N T I A N   M O U N T A I N S

Lake Nipigon

St. Lawrence

Nova Scotia

Lake Superior

L. Michigan   Lake Huron

90°   80°   70°   60°

40°

A cotton field in the warm south-eastern region of the United States, with ripening bolls of hairy seeds. The trees are yellow buckeye (left, with flowers inset), southern catalpa (centre) and pecan (right, with nut and kernel inset).

given its name by woodsmen who thought that its foliage had the same rank smell as the very different European hemlock plant. The hemlock's attractive, dark-green foliage is built up of small needles of irregular lengths. Its softwood timber has many industrial uses, mainly as packaging or paper-pulp, and its bark, rich in tannin, has long been used for turning hides into leather.

Late in spring the bushy flowering dogwood tree opens its white or pink flower heads above its foliage of rich-green, oval, paired leaves. Each head displays four large bracts in the shape of a single flower, but the structures at the centre, which look like stamens, are actually clustered blossoms, and the bracts serve as flags to attract insects to them.

Along the banks of streams is found the wild American persimmon, one of several native trees that bear edible, succulent fruits. Four-petalled yellow flowers open amid its foliage of simple oval leaves. The fruit, which may be yellow, red, or orange, is two inches across and resembles a tomato; it has a delicious juicy flesh around its central stone. On open ground along the fringes of lakes and bogs grows the highbush blueberry, so-called to differentiate it from lower shrubs bearing

similar blue fruit. It is an evergreen with tough wiry stems, round leathery leaves, and bell-shaped, pink flowers.

Woodland clearings and waste lands are often colonized by the evening primrose, a biennial that has very small, easily-scattered seeds. It draws its name from its yellow flowers, which open as the sun sets and are usually pollinated by night-flying moths, attracted by the strong fragrance. In swamps and woodland openings grows the brilliant Canada lily. It springs from a bulb deep in the ground, and sends up its tall stem, bearing whorls of oval leaves, late in spring.

Another bright flower of swamps and moist broad-leaved woods is the showy lady's slipper orchid, which also springs from a deep bulbous rootstock. The slipper shape of its pink-and-white flower is a device to ensure cross-pollination. Insects that enter the blossom usually try to escape by crawling up the rim of the large, rounded lower petal. But it is cunningly bent over and they fall back again. Eventually they find the only escape route, between the stamens and the pistil, and by following this they brush pollen from another flower on to the stigma, and pick up fresh pollen to carry to another plant.

Waterside plants of America's southern states. Honey locust trees (left) thrive along streamsides: red iris (below) and pickerel weed (right) come up each spring, through shallow water, from rootstocks anchored in the mud.

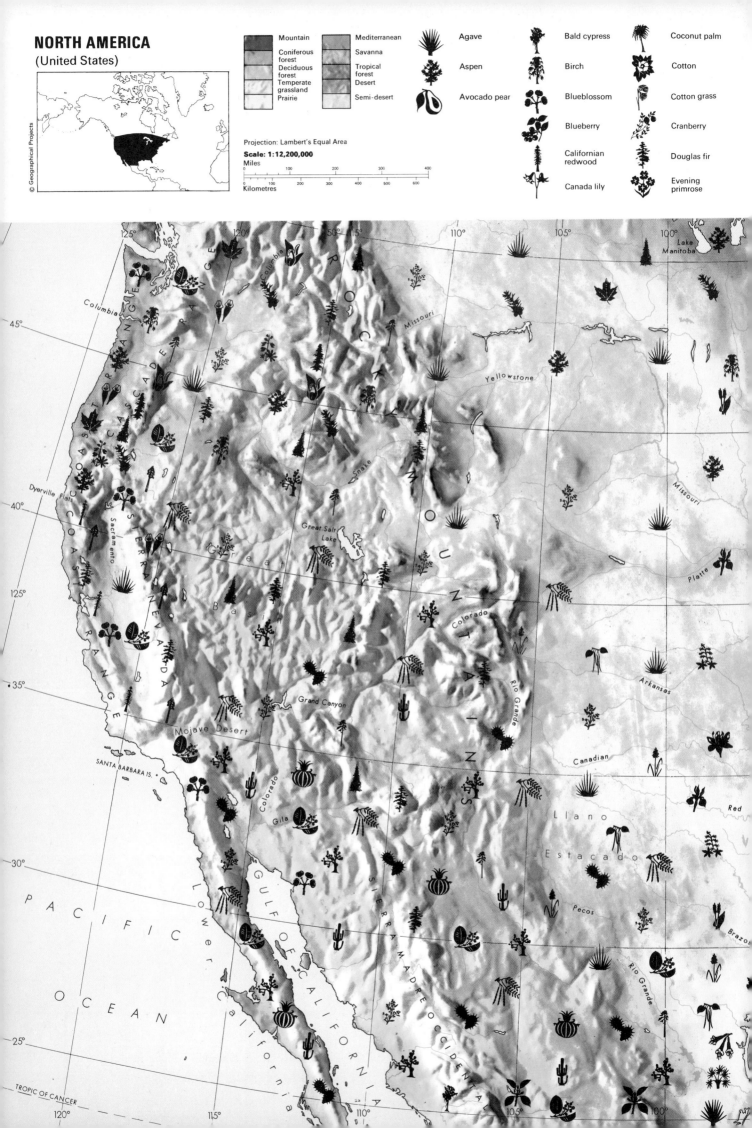

NORTH AMERICA
(United States)

© Geographical Projects

Mountain		Mediterranean	
Coniferous forest		Savanna	
Deciduous forest		Tropical forest	
Temperate grassland		Desert	
Prairie		Semi-desert	

Agave
Aspen
Avocado pear

Bald cypress
Birch
Blueblossom
Blueberry
Californian redwood
Canada lily

Coconut palm
Cotton
Cotton grass
Cranberry
Douglas fir
Evening primrose

Projection: Lambert's Equal Area

Scale: 1:12,200,000

Miles
0   100   200   300   400

Kilometres
0   100   200   300   400   500   600

PACIFIC OCEAN

TROPIC OF CANCER

Flowering dogwood
Giant sequoia
Hemlock
Honey locust
Jamaica thatchpalm
Joshua tree

Juniper
Kentucky bluegrass
Madrone
Mahogany
Maple
Mescal button cactus

Mesquite
Pasture grass
Pecan
Persimmon
Pickerel weed
Pine

Pitcher plant (Sarracenia)
Poinsettia
Prickly pear
Red iris
Red oak
Sagebrush

Saguaro
Saw palmetto
Showy lady's slipper orchid
Skunk cabbage
Snakemouth flower
Southern catalpa

Southern magnolia
Spruce
Trumpet-creeper
Wild lupin
Yellow buckeye
Yellow water lily

The southern states that reach from the broad basin of the Mississippi towards the warm Atlantic Ocean have warmer summers with ample rainfall. Their characteristic trees and plants include many fascinating kinds. The southern catalpa, for example, strikes a tropical note when it opens its blossoms in July. Each trumpet-shaped flower has an uneven-sided, frilled white corolla of united petals, blotched with purple and brown. They ripen to slender, hanging black seed-pods which, because their supposed medicinal properties were known to the Indians, have earned this tree the name of "Indian bean."

On woodland edges grows the yellow buckeye, which bears large compound leaves similar to those of the closely related European horse chestnut. Spikes of bright yellow flowers appear on the tree each June. Its nut, which has a white patch on a deep brown ground, is supposed to resemble the eye of a wild deer or buck.

Wild pecan trees, relatives of the walnuts and hickories, are the source of many cultivated strains grown in southern orchards. They have long compound leaves, and their flowers, which open in May, are catkin-like. The male flowers look like lamb's tails, while the female ones are flask-shaped. The latter ripen to delicious pecan nuts, best described as smooth-shelled walnuts with a finer flavour. The bark is shaggy, and the timber tough and durable.

Cotton, a leading economic field crop in the south, is derived in large degree from native American wild cotton plants that were known to the Indians before European settlement began, although some varieties have an Old World origin. Cotton is grown as an annual on fertile, well-cultivated land, and is

Southern magnolia, a bushy evergreen tree, bears large, glossy, drought-resistant leaves and big, globe-shaped white blossoms.

planted in rows for ease of weeding and harvesting. The shrubby plants bear masses of bell-shaped blossoms in midsummer, these being yellow, white or pink according to strain. They quickly ripen to hard brown seed-pods, or bolls, which split to release the tiny seeds, each attached to a mass of fluffy white cotton hairs. For 300 years the cotton bolls were gathered singly by hand, a heavy task for thousands of plantation workers. Today, tall tractor-drawn machines pluck them rapidly from the stems. Other machines remove the husks and the seeds, leaving the fine, twisted white seed-hairs, which go to the mills to be manufactured into thread and cloth.

Drier and poorer land is often left under grass, as pastures and meadows. The Kentucky bluegrass, so called from the shade of its long leaf-blades, is a particularly valuable kind, since the deep-going roots that spread out from its tussocks resist drought.

The many streams that wander over these broad plains have their attractive waterside vegetation, amongst which is the honey locust tree. This tree gained its odd name because it reminded early colonists of John the Baptist's diet of honey and wild locusts in the wilderness. Its fragrant white flowers are rich in nectar, and its seed-pods hold a soft sweet pulp that makes them palatable, to both men and animals. It is found over a wide area of central and eastern United States and is often cultivated as a shade tree because of its attractive foliage. Each leaf is doubly compound, having leaflets that are themselves made up of leaflet-clusters. The twigs carry sharp spines in groups of three, which check browsing deer.

In marshes and along the sides of streams grows the stately red iris, which passes the winter as a stout rootstock, deep below water level. In summer it sends up clumps of sword-shaped leaves, topped by large flowers with spreading petals. A smaller, more truly aquatic plant is the pickerel weed, which is anchored in the mud just off the shore and opens pale-green leaves shaped like arrow-heads that project above the water surface. In midsummer it bears club-shaped spikes of clear blue flowers.

Near the Atlantic seaboard of the southern states, the low summer rainfall combines with high temperatures to limit the leading plants to kinds especially adapted to resist drought. The long-leaf pine thrives and grows very quickly on arid sandy soils. Its trunk is often tapped to gain the resin and turpentine—known locally as "naval stores"—that ooze from the wounded wood. When the trees are eventually felled for lumber or paper pulp, the cleared land is rapidly recolonized by seedlings springing from the dispersed winged seeds that ripen in the pines' large cones.

The ground below the pines supports a sparse growth of the saw palmetto, a low plant with fan-shaped leaves and sharp spines on the leaf-stalks. This dwarf palm owes its survival to its spiky protection. Larger leaves, suitable for thatching, are borne by the Jamaican thatchpalm, a slender stately tree that carries clusters of yellow flowers and bunches of white fruits.

Many of the smaller trees and shrubs, such as the "live" oaks, are evergreen. Their tough leathery leaves, glossy dark-green above and paler below, are adapted to retain moisture in a climate that includes occasional winter frost, spring drought, and intense summer heat. One of the most striking plants is the southern magnolia, which bears huge oval leaves and large cup-shaped flowers with many free, pinkish-white petals, opening in May. It is often grown in more northern gardens either as a bush or as a vigorous climber on a south-facing wall.

The many swamps, lakes, and sluggish streams of the south-east support a remarkable conifer called the swamp cypress (*Taxodium distichum*). It is also called the "bald cypress" because it loses all its leaves each winter, when it can no longer draw moisture from the mud set solid in the frozen streams. Its leaves turn a vivid coppery orange in the autumn and fall in groups of a few needles each. Swamp cypress shows the rare feature of air-roots, which are also called "pneumatophores" or "knees." These knobbly structures grow upwards into the air from the submerged roots, and carry life-giving oxygen down to them. The timber, which is strong, reddish-brown, fragrant, and durable, is often harvested for fine joinery and greenhouse construction, since it resists damp. Swamp cypresses are often festooned with the so-called "Spanish moss," which is not a moss but an epiphytic higher plant with tufted leaves that eventually become ragged and trail down from the branches.

The many lianas, or climbing plants, that trail over the stems of Florida's shrubs and trees include the trumpet-creeper, a member of the bignonia family. It displays large, orange, trumpet-shaped flowers each August. The little snakemouth flower adds a touch of bright mauve to the bog vegetation of sedge, moss, and grass. Related to the orchids, it draws its name from the resemblance of the flower to a snake's mouth.

Only plants adapted to hot, dry conditions can thrive in Arizona's torrid deserts. The Joshua tree (far left) bears tufts of sharp, slender leaves at the tips of much-branched stems. Beneath it grows sagebrush, which provides scanty fodder for rangers' cattle. Prickly pear (centre foreground) is a cactus whose juicy stems, armed with spines to check browsing, do the work of leaves.

Beyond the Mississippi river the prairies extend west towards the Rocky Mountains, north to the Canadian sprucewoods, and south to the semi-deserts of the Mexican border. Their constant features are cold winters, hot, sunny summers, and a low rainfall that is adequate to support grass and grain, though insufficient for forests. Fortunately for the wheat farmers, the rain falls mainly during spring and early summer, which is the growing season for grain. Dry weather prevails during the months of ripening and harvesting. The prevailing natural cover of wild pasture grasses once supported herds of buffalo, and the fires lit by Indian hunters checked all other forms of plant life, though grasses survived.

The American states of the Pacific north-west, together with British Columbia and south Alaska, form the world's best example of a temperate rain forest. The strong prevailing south-west winds, blowing in across the full width of the Pacific Ocean, are obliged to ascend the Rocky Mountains. The resulting cooling causes frequent downpours of relatively warm rain, almost the whole year round. Clouds are frequent, humidity is consistently high. These moist conditions, with hot summers and mild winters, prove ideal for the growth of the world's tallest and largest trees.

Current height records are held by the Californian, or coast, redwoods. They are stout trees with very thick, soft, ridged, fibrous bark, and evergreen foliage closely resembling that of yew. The coast redwood bears tiny catkin-like flowers of both sexes on the same tree, and ripens knobbly brown cones holding minute winged seeds. It is the leading tree of the coastal "fog belt" of California, where its strong durable timber is used by a major lumber industry. The finest specimens are today preserved in national parks. The tallest recorded redwood, located on the Dyerville Flats, 33 miles south-west of Eureka, measured 364 feet high. The stoutest, at Crescent City, also in California, is 66 feet around. Ring counts have shown that some redwood trees are over 2,000 years old. Though redwood has been introduced to most temperate lands as a vigorous ornamental tree, it is rarely grown outside California for its lumber.

Another striking Pacific coast tree is the Douglas fir, so called because the exploring Scottish botanist David Douglas introduced its seeds to Europe in 1827. This conifer (*Pseudotsuga menziesii*) has a very strong timber with marked annual rings, which is marketed as Oregon or British Columbian "pine." It is now widely planted in Scotland, western Europe, Australia, and New Zealand, wherever the climate matches that of its mountainous homeland. It may grow 300 feet tall and up to 30 feet around, and stand for 300 years; one record-breaker, felled at Vancouver in 1895, was 417 feet high!

On the heavily shaded forest floor below redwoods and firs, only a handful of flowering plants and shrubs can survive. Much of the ground is encumbered by decaying tree trunks, and the sparse undergrowth consists largely of tall ferns and lowly mosses. The blueblossoms, or Californian lilacs, occur widely as shrubs or climbers. Some are evergreen and others are deciduous, and most kinds open attractive sprays of bright

Giant saguaro cactuses (right) stand like sentinels; their leafless stems bear spines along every rib. An agave (centre) sends up a tall flower-spike from a tuft of sword-shaped leaves. The shrubby madrone (middle distance, right of centre) bears evergreen foliage and white flower clusters. The mesquite (far right) is a spiny bush. Mescal button cactus (right foreground) forms a low cushion with one central bloom.

NORTH AMERICA
(Mexico & Central America)

© Geographical Projects

■	Mountain		Prairie
	Coniferous forest		Savanna
	Deciduous forest		Tropical forest
	Temperate grassland		Desert

Semi-desert

Projection: Lambert's Equal Area

Scale: 1:14,300,000

Miles
0 100 200 300 400

Kilometres
0 100 200 300 400 500 600 700

Agave		Cotton	
Avocado pear		Dahlia	
Bald cypress		Douglas fir	
Canna		Honey locust	
Coconut palm		Jamaica thatchpalm	

Joshua tree

Kentucky bluegrass

Madrone

Mahogany

Mescal button cactus

Mesquite

Pasture grass

Pecan

Persimmon

Pickerel wee

Pine

Poinsettia

Prickly pear

Red iris

Sagebrush

Saguaro

Saw palmetto

Snakemouth flower

Southern catalpa

Southern magnolia

Strawberry

Sunflower

Trumpet-creeper

Yellow buckeye

ATLANTIC

OCEAN

TROPIC OF CANCER

BAHAMA ISLANDS

WEST INDIES

STR. OF FLORIDA

Ever-glades

TURKS & CAICOS IS.

LEEWARD

PUERTO RICO

ISLANDS

HISPANIOLA

GREATER

CUBA

ANTILLES

LESSER

CAYMAN IS.

JAMAICA

ANTILLES

WINDWARD ISLANDS

CARIBBEAN

SEA

Limit of North American region

SOUTH

Isthmus of Panama

GULF OF PANAMA

AMERICA

blue flowers in the spring and again in autumn. Along slow, shallow streams grows the foul-smelling skunk cabbage, which is related to the arum lilies. A perennial with a fleshy rootstock, it opens a large, fleshy, bright yellow spathe in spring. At the centre of this is a pale-yellow flower-spike carrying separate clusters of male and female flowers.

Shingle banks formed by swift-flowing rivers are often colonized by the blue wild lupin. Seeds floating downstream become stranded on gravel, germinate and form a network of roots that help to hold the stones in place. The nodules on these roots fix nitrogen from the air, and the decay of nitrogen-rich plant tissues slowly creates a fertile soil. Unless a strong flood follows, the shingle bank may become a permanent island. The lupin bears its numerous sweet-pea-shaped flowers in tall upright spikes. When the black seed-pods ripen they open with an explosive twist, scattering the seeds around the parent plant and into the river.

These dense woods hold many nooks and crannies where plants cannot send their roots through the mass of decaying wood, foliage, and peat down to the original soil. Often the seedlings of giant timber trees, including the western red cedar (*Thuja plicata*) that the Indians used for their totem poles, and the magnificent Sitka spruce, start life in decaying bark on the top of a fallen log.

In marshes full of plant debris plants may be unable to win enough nitrogen from the soil below. Hence these forests hold a small group of insectivorous plants that have modified some of their leaves to form an open tube, or pitcher, as in the American pitcher plant, *Sarracenia*. Insects that fly or stumble into this pitcher fail to climb out over its incurved rim. They eventually fall into the pool of digestive liquid that the plant has secreted at the bottom. There they drown, and their dead tissues provide the nitrogen that the plant so badly needs.

In a few small isolated groves amid the mountains of California grows the mammoth tree, or giant sequoia, also called the wellingtonia. Botanically, it is closely related to the coast redwood, but has spiky, pale-green foliage. The world's stoutest trees, these mammoths measure up to 75 feet around, and some scale over 300 feet tall. Counts of annual rings reveal ages up to 3,000 years. Giant sequoia timber is strong and sound, but there are too few trees to support a lumber trade and most are preserved as national monuments.

I n the central and southern sections of the western United States, and neighbouring parts of Mexico, there is a vast tract of desert and semi-desert country. The summers are hot and dry and what little rain there is falls mostly in the winter. Only plants that are specially adapted to resist drought can survive. Many are armed with spines to protect them from the grazing animals that can find no normal herbage to eat.

True trees are rare, though this region is the home of one of the world's longest-lived trees, the scrubby bristle-cone pine; this may persist, growing infinitely slowly, for 5,000 years. On the torrid plains near the Mexican border the picturesque

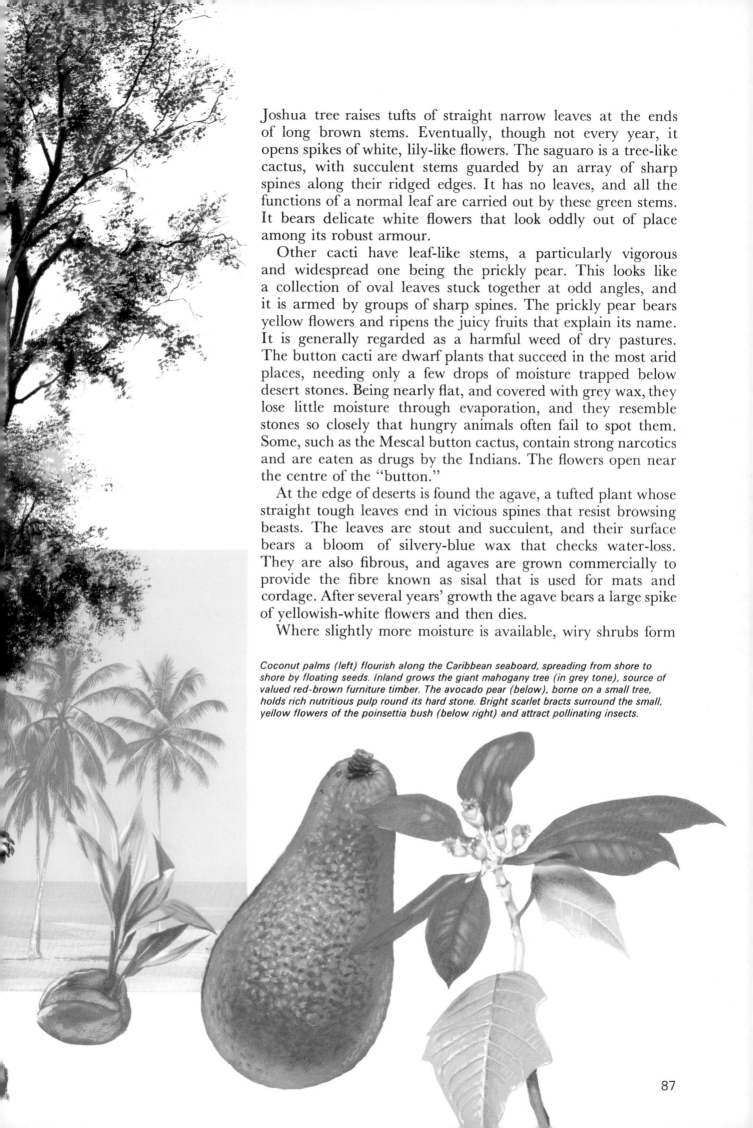

Joshua tree raises tufts of straight narrow leaves at the ends of long brown stems. Eventually, though not every year, it opens spikes of white, lily-like flowers. The saguaro is a tree-like cactus, with succulent stems guarded by an array of sharp spines along their ridged edges. It has no leaves, and all the functions of a normal leaf are carried out by these green stems. It bears delicate white flowers that look oddly out of place among its robust armour.

Other cacti have leaf-like stems, a particularly vigorous and widespread one being the prickly pear. This looks like a collection of oval leaves stuck together at odd angles, and it is armed by groups of sharp spines. The prickly pear bears yellow flowers and ripens the juicy fruits that explain its name. It is generally regarded as a harmful weed of dry pastures. The button cacti are dwarf plants that succeed in the most arid places, needing only a few drops of moisture trapped below desert stones. Being nearly flat, and covered with grey wax, they lose little moisture through evaporation, and they resemble stones so closely that hungry animals often fail to spot them. Some, such as the Mescal button cactus, contain strong narcotics and are eaten as drugs by the Indians. The flowers open near the centre of the "button."

At the edge of deserts is found the agave, a tufted plant whose straight tough leaves end in vicious spines that resist browsing beasts. The leaves are stout and succulent, and their surface bears a bloom of silvery-blue wax that checks water-loss. They are also fibrous, and agaves are grown commercially to provide the fibre known as sisal that is used for mats and cordage. After several years' growth the agave bears a large spike of yellowish-white flowers and then dies.

Where slightly more moisture is available, wiry shrubs form

Coconut palms (left) flourish along the Caribbean seaboard, spreading from shore to shore by floating seeds. Inland grows the giant mahogany tree (in grey tone), source of valued red-brown furniture timber. The avocado pear (below), borne on a small tree, holds rich nutritious pulp round its hard stone. Bright scarlet bracts surround the small, yellow flowers of the poinsettia bush (below right) and attract pollinating insects.

87

low ground cover. One is the mesquite, a spiny bush that bears spikes of yellow flowers shaped like sweet peas. Another is the sagebrush, which has greyish flowers and provides a meagre source of food for the ranchers' cattle. A third, the madrone, has glossy evergreen leaves that make good use of winter rainfall yet resist summer drought. Its stems are clad in red, peeling bark and it bears, in autumn, bunches of bell-shaped, waxy white blossoms. These take a whole year to ripen into the fruit, a red globe of soft flesh resembling a strawberry.

Along the sun-drenched shores of Central America and the West Indies grows the coconut palm, a tree adapted to spread, by seed, across the tropical oceans. Its hard, round nut ripens within a much larger oval husk composed of a light, tough fibre. This falls intact from the tree and acts as a float, allowing the seed to travel safely for hundreds of miles along ocean currents. The sweet milk and nutritious flesh within the coconut shell are a valuable food resource for the people of coastal communities. They use the coarse fibres of the husks for matting and the huge leaves to make rainproof walls and roofs.

On the drier soils inland many tall timber trees thrive under the adequate, though seasonal, rainfall. Mahogany, the largest and commercially most valuable of these, forms a stately bole over 150 feet high and 40 feet around, strengthened by broad buttresses at its base. The strong, easily worked timber was first used by the Indians, who hollowed out tree trunks to make canoes. From the 1500's onwards it has been regularly exported for furniture making, fine joinery, and shipbuilding.

Many wild plants of the Central American zone have gained a place in cultivation either because of their beauty or their merit as food crops. One of these is the avocado pear, a bushy tree with greenish-yellow flowers that bears clusters of pear-shaped fruits clothed in a tough, dark-green skin. Within this, and surrounding the single hard seed, lies a thick layer of nutritious yellowish-white flesh, rich in fat and protein. A Central American plant renowned for its beauty is the poinsettia, which is a member of the spurge group, its stems holding the white milky juice which is their characteristic feature. It is cultivated in tropical gardens, as well as in temperate greenhouses, for the striking beauty of its red flower bracts. These attract pollinating insects to the flowers, which are greenish-yellow and inconspicuous.

The wild dahlia, native to Mexico, is a low perennial plant with pale-mauve, daisy-shaped flowers, that passes the cold winter as a clump of fleshy tubers hidden beneath the soil. The Indians occasionally gather these tubers to eat, cooking them like potatoes, and this led to the dahlia's introduction to Europe as a possible food crop. European gardeners found it more attractive as a decorative plant and it was speedily developed into a host of varieties, with flowers of exceptional shapes in a full range of colours. Cannas, with their brilliant orange, red, or purple blossoms, provide another example of a Central American plant cultivated in temperate-zone gardens. They shoot up vigorously during the summer, bearing bold

Mexico has contributed valuable flower and food plants to the world's fields and gardens. The giant annual sunflower (top) is grown both for decoration and for its oil-producing seeds. Wild dahlia (right) is the parent of countless showy ornamental kinds. Cannas (far right) add brilliance to tropical flower-beds. Cultivated strawberries (bottom right) are derived from wild Mexican species.

flower-spikes amid clusters of broad, sword-shaped leaves. But autumn brings an end to their display, and their tender bulbs, like cultivated dahlia tubers, need frost-proof protection through the winter.

Wild Mexican strawberries are the parent strains of many cultivated varieties. They grow naturally on seashores and sandbanks, where their runners or rooting stems enable them to spread over unstable bare ground. Once established, each rooted clump bears three-lobed leaves, with clusters of white blossoms that quickly ripen into fruits. From Mexico, also comes the tall sunflower, a sturdy annual plant now grown in Europe, Africa, and North America as a field crop for its oil-producing seeds. The oval, flattish, grey-and-white seeds are sown in spring, and the plants grow with amazing speed to heights of nine feet or more. Each stem bears large oval leaves and is topped, in late summer, by a huge yellow compound flower, shaped like a symbolic sun. This flower's central disc, composed of tubular florets, is surrounded by several rows of the showy, aptly named, ray florets. The ray florets, being sterile, serve only to attract visiting bees. The functional tubular florets reward them with nectar.

89

6 South America

Amazon jungles, home of mahogany, Brazil nut, and giant water lily. Argentine pampas grasses and quaint Andean desert cacti. World food plants from South America: potato, maize, cassava, and peanut.

With the exception of local variations in the high tablelands of the Andes Mountains and on the broad plateaus of Brazil and Guyana, South America shows a regular succession of climatic zones from north to south, with regional extremes of temperature and rainfall, though moderate seasonal changes. In the north, a broad expanse of the continent lies across the Equator and has a tropical climate. By contrast, the narrow peninsula of Tierra del Fuego at the southernmost tip of Patagonia is a windswept wilderness of rock, with snowy mountains.

The South American tropical rain forests, or selvas, extend for 2,000 miles across the northern bulge of the continent, from the Andes Mountains in the west to the Atlantic Ocean in the east. For the most part they occupy the basin of the Amazon River, which, with its many tributaries, winds slowly over a vast flood plain towards the sea. Rainfall is fairly constant around the year, but any excess causes flooding and the tallest and sturdiest trees are adapted to these conditions. The silk-cotton tree, for example, develops with age a huge bole, supported by plank-like buttresses projecting at its base that spread the weight over a large area of soft soil. It bears large, pinkish-white flowers that ripen large seed-pods. Inside the pods every small seed has a tuft of cotton-like hairs. This downy material, called kapok, will not make good cloth, but is widely used for lining winter clothing, and in life-jackets, because it keeps in heat and resists moisture.

Other leading rain-forest trees are mahogany, greenheart—which has great natural strength and durability and is used for dock and harbour construction—and several species of *Bombax*. These very large waterside trees are hollowed out by the Indians to make dug-out canoes. A smaller timber tree of high commercial value is the Brazilian rosewood. It has feathery, compound leaves built up of many small leaflets and bears

Brazilian rain forest. Silk-cotton trees soar from buttressed stumps. Epiphytes, rooting on branches, include vriesia (right) and scrambling ceriman (left). Flamingo flowers (lower right) display red, heart-shaped bracts. Amazon water lilies float huge round leaves and starry blossoms on the river's surface.

sprays of yellow flowers, each shaped like a sweet-pea blossom. Rosewood's attractions lie in the smooth even texture of its dense wood, which fit it for the most precise cabinet-making and carving. It is a rich warm brown in colour, with an intricate graining of black streaks. The name of rosewood comes from its fragrance, for it smells of rose blossoms when freshly cut.

Many trees in this moist rain forest carry epiphytes. Typical of these are the vriesias, which are often grown as pot plants in centrally-heated houses in temperate lands. Each leaf has a curved base that clasps the leaf within it, and at the same time forms a cup to catch rainwater. The ceriman, which bears the expressive scientific name of *Monstera deliciosa*, begins life as an epiphyte but is able to send down long fleshy trailing roots that may make contact with the ground. It bears huge, drooping leaves that are unique for their natural development of holes in the leaf-blade. Many suggestions have been made about the purpose of these holes, one being that they provide for the rapid drying-out of the leaf-blade's surface, since the ceriman often starts life low down near the forest floor and could suffer from an excess of rain, mist, and leaf-drip. It climbs upwards by extending leafy shoots that develop, just behind their tips, stiff aerial roots that support them on tree branches. The exquisite morning glory, or ipomoea, is a smaller, true tree-climbing plant, rooted in the ground, which twines around slender stems and opens, at daybreak, deep-blue, trumpet-shaped blossoms.

Low on the forest floor grows the flamingo flower, which is often seen in cultivation as a pot plant. The bright red "petal" that appears to be a flower is actually a large bract that serves to attract insects. The flowers are grouped along a pink spike that has a fanciful resemblance to the neck of a flamingo.

On surfaces of shallow lakes and slow-moving rivers float the enormous leaves of the giant Amazon water lily. The leaves spring up from the rootstock embedded in the ooze at the bottom and grow rapidly thanks to the ample warmth, moisture, and nutrients. When fully expanded, a single leaf—the world's largest—may be three feet across. It has a network of huge veins and an upturned rim to give added strength. One leaf can support, on the water surface, the weight of a small child. The flowers, starry, pale-pink lilies with many petals, open just clear of the water, and may become 18 inches wide.

Though the tropical forests of South America yield only a scanty sustenance of fruits and nuts to the roving Indians, they are the source of several trees valued under cultivation. Cocoa is a leading example, though today the main commercial crops are grown in West Africa. It is a small tree with large, drooping, evergreen, leathery leaves, adapted to live under constant moisture in the shade of taller trees. It bears clusters of pink, star-shaped flowers directly on its main trunk and larger branches. The flowers ripen into large red or yellow oval pods, which are harvested and split open to secure the white seeds, or cocoa beans. These are scooped out and fermented in heaps covered by banana leaves. During this process the beans turn dull red and develop the delicious flavour we enjoy in chocolate

The Pará rubber tree (right) originated beneath the shade of taller trees in Brazil's Amazon jungles; it is now grown extensively in tropical Asia. Here an Indian woman tapper freshens a shallow cut in the bark with a sharp chisel. White latex gum flows down, following a spout to a cup. Each day the tapper collects two full buckets of milky fluid, for conversion to rubber.

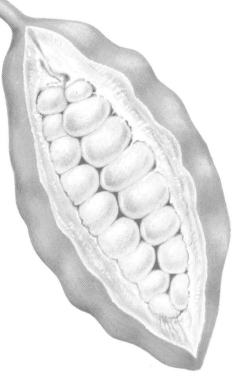

and cocoa. Next the beans are roasted and the shells crushed to release the tasty kernels.

Another commercially important tree native to South America is the Brazil nut, which is a larger tree that claims a place in the upper storey of the rain forest. It has large, oval, dull-green leaves, up to two feet long, and creamy yellow flowers, which are followed by big woody capsules each holding many closely packed triangular nuts. One wild, fruit-bearing tree that has gained wide acceptance, and which is now cultivated in many tropical countries, is the guava. It bears pale-green, oval leaves and white, waxy flowers, followed by juicy, oval, yellow fruits holding pink pulp and many pale-yellow seeds. The guava's piquant flavour makes it a popular dessert fruit, and it is also canned for export or made into jam.

The pará rubber tree plays only a small part in the great forests, though a major one in world commerce. A tree of medium size, it persists amid the larger kinds because it is able to tolerate deep shade. Throughout the tree runs a system of latex canals, and if any part of the tree is damaged this latex oozes out at once as a white milky fluid. Within a few hours this

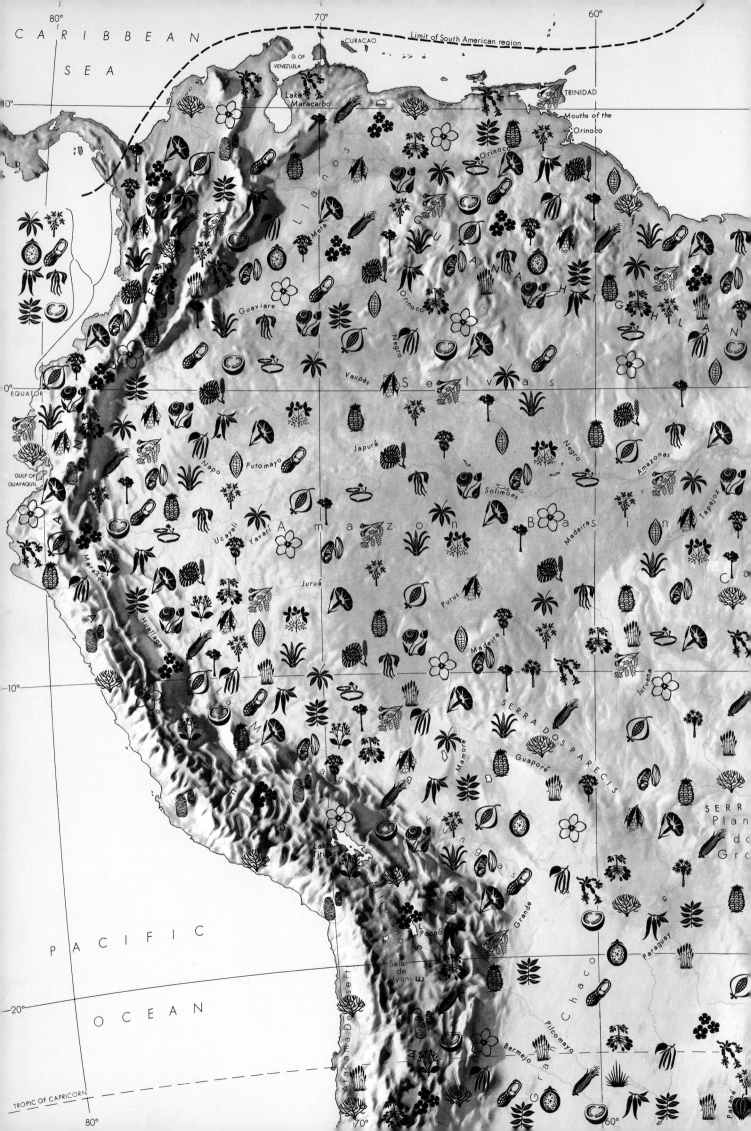

CARIBBEAN
SEA

80°

70°

60°

Limit of South American region

CURAÇAO

G. OF
VENEZUELA

Lake
Maracaibo

TRINIDAD

Mouths of the
Orinoco

10°

Orinoco

L l a n o s

G U I A N A   H I G H L A N D S

Meta

Guaviare

Orinoco

Negro

Vaupés

S e l v a s

0°

EQUATOR

Japurá

Negro

Amazonas

Napo

Putomayo

Solimões

GULF OF
GUAYAQUIL

A m a z o n   B a s i n

Ucayali

Yavari

Tapajoz

Marañón

Juruá

Purus

Madeiras

Huallaga

Madeira

Juruena

10°

S E R R A   D O S   P A R E C I S

Mamoré

Guaporé

SERR
Plan
do
Gr

Lake
Titicaca

PACIFIC

Poopó

Grande

Paraguay

Salar
de
Uyuni

20°

OCEAN

Atacama Desert

C h a c o

Bermejo

Pilcomayo

TROPIC OF CAPRICORN

Paraná

80°

70°

60°

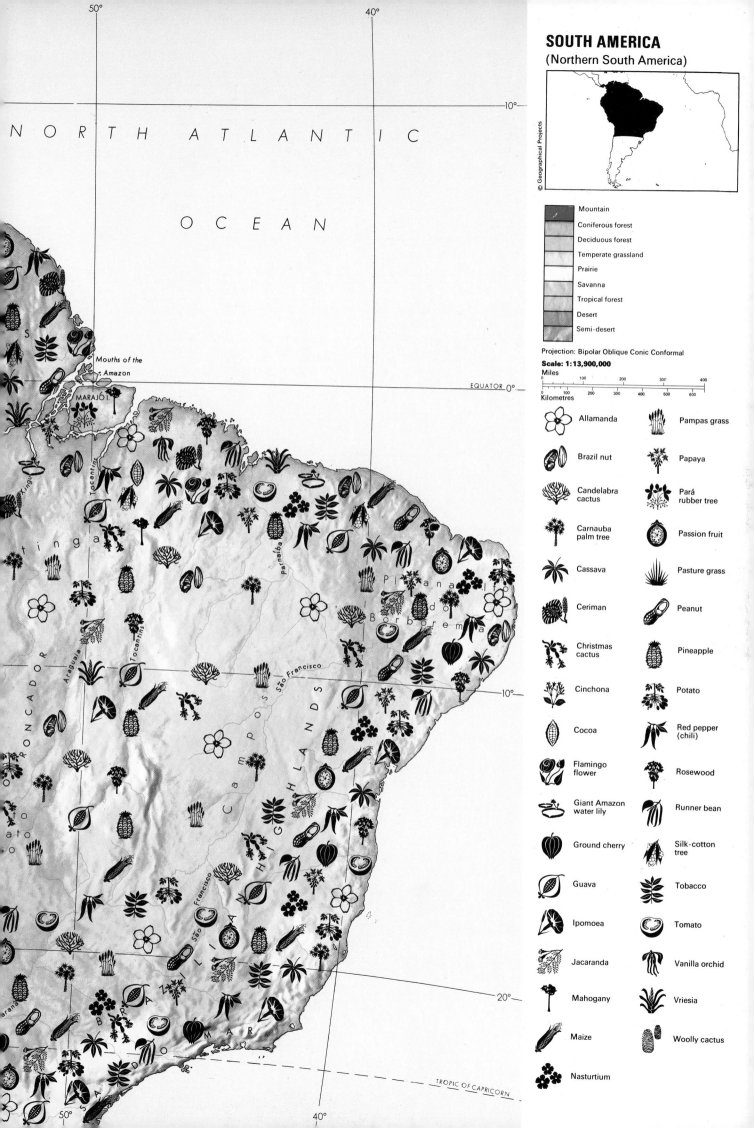

SOUTH AMERICA
(Northern South America)

© Geographical Projects

Mountain
Coniferous forest
Deciduous forest
Temperate grassland
Prairie
Savanna
Tropical forest
Desert
Semi-desert

Projection: Bipolar Oblique Conic Conformal

Scale: 1:13,900,000

Miles
0   100   200   300   400

Kilometres
0   100   200   300   400   500   600

Allamanda	Pampas grass	
Brazil nut	Papaya	
Candelabra cactus	Pará rubber tree	
Carnauba palm tree	Passion fruit	
Cassava	Pasture grass	
Ceriman	Peanut	
Christmas cactus	Pineapple	
Cinchona	Potato	
Cocoa	Red pepper (chili)	
Flamingo flower	Rosewood	
Giant Amazon water lily	Runner bean	
Ground cherry	Silk-cotton tree	
Guava	Tobacco	
Ipomoea	Tomato	
Jacaranda	Vanilla orchid	
Mahogany	Vriesia	
Maize	Woolly cactus	
Nasturtium		

coagulates into a skin of rubber over the cut, sealing the wound against attack by insects or invasion by fungi.

Rubber was first gathered by the Indians as a curiosity, and used to make balls and playthings. In the mid-1800's, the possible uses of rubber were greatly increased by the development of vulcanization, a chemical process that made the natural latex more stable and durable. The resulting world demand could not be met from the South American forests, where there were too few workers to establish commercial plantations. The British Government therefore commissioned Sir Henry Wickham to bring the seeds of rubber trees out of Brazil to make cultivation possible elsewhere. The rubber plantations that were quickly established in Sri Lanka, Malaysia, and Indonesia soon exceeded the natural forests in output and met the enormous demand for rubber trees that came with developing motor transport.

Several trees have been selected from the South American jungles for ornamental cultivation. The best known is the jacaranda, now planted as a street or garden tree in many tropical and sub-tropical cities. It has an annual outburst of brilliant violet-blue blossoms that almost hide its crown of feathery foliage. The allamanda bush has likewise been planted in most tropical countries for its gay display of bright-yellow, trumpet-shaped flowers.

The northern, tropical region of South America is the original home not only of many valuable trees but also of several food plants that are now cultivated throughout the world's tropics. The cassava plant, for example, which is also known as tapioca, has become a staple food for peasant cultivators in West Africa and Malaysia. It is a tall jungle plant with compound leaves that have several leaflets radiating like the fingers of a hand. The cassava plant has small, greenish flowers, and grows steadily the whole year round and so can be harvested at any season. It builds up a clump of large, fleshy tubers, rich in starch, which, however, contain a poisonous juice and cannot be eaten raw. The American Indians eliminated this poison by squeezing the pulped tubers in baskets; today its potency is overcome by prolonged boiling. The tapioca used in milk puddings is made by rasping the tubers, filtering out the starch grains and forming them into small, round balls by roasting.

The papaya, or pawpaw *(Carica papaya)*, is a soft-stemmed, tree-like plant that grows very fast in its tropical savanna home. Its oval fruits, each the size of a football, are bright yellow and hold soft, orange-yellow, pleasant-tasting pulp. They are borne in dense clusters directly on the stout upright stem. By contrast, the pineapple, which is also native to tropical South America, bears fruits close to the ground. The pineapple plant starts life by forming a tuft of stout, bluish-green, sword-shaped leaves, edged with spines to discourage grazing animals. Once established, it sends up, from its fleshy rootstock, a central flowering shoot that bears small, greenish-mauve flowers. After pollination, the bracts at the flower-bases swell, turn yellow, and grow together to form the familiar, fine-flavoured, juicy fruit.

The peanut, or groundnut, which originates in northern

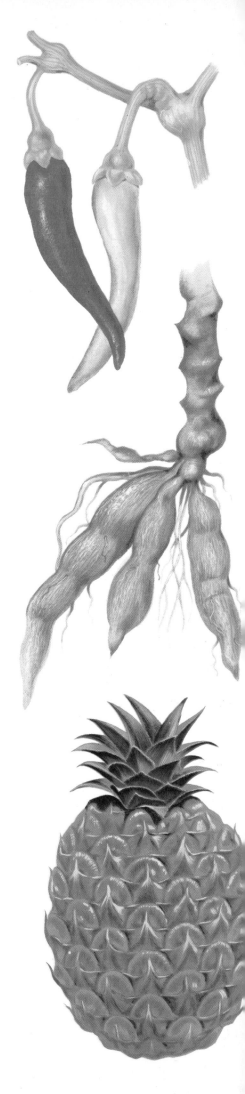

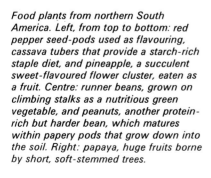

Food plants from northern South America. Left, from top to bottom: red pepper seed-pods used as flavouring, cassava tubers that provide a starch-rich staple diet, and pineapple, a succulent sweet-flavoured flower cluster, eaten as a fruit. Centre: runner beans, grown on climbing stalks as a nutritious green vegetable, and peanuts, another protein-rich but harder bean, which matures within papery pods that grow down into the soil. Right: papaya, huge fruits borne by short, soft-stemmed trees.

South America and is now cultivated in most tropical lands, has the remarkable habit of burying its own seeds in the soil. A low plant with compound leaves, it bears white flowers shaped like sweet peas. As these develop into pale-brown, tough-skinned pods, the stems bearing them turn downwards and force the pods into the soft earth, from which they are eventually harvested. Like other members of its family, the Leguminoseae, the peanut has nodules on its roots that enable it to fix nitrogen from the air. Much of this nitrogen is transferred to its seeds, or peanuts, which form a protein-rich food of great value to their peasant cultivators.

Another South American legume is the scarlet runner bean, a climber that grows rapidly in warm weather. Its long seed-pods are gathered while they are still soft and green, before they have transferred the full share of nourishment to the oval, pink and black beans developing within. In the tropics, the runner bean, which forms a fleshy tuber below ground, grows all the year round, but in temperate countries it is grown as an annual from seed.

Flavourings, too, can be obtained from many tropical South American plants. One that has gained a universal place in cookery throughout the world is vanilla from the vanilla orchid. This is a frail climbing plant that grows up the stems of rain forest trees, clinging to them by aerial roots. It has glossy, pale-green leaves, and opens clusters of white blossoms that ripen to slender, hanging, green seed-pods. These contain the powerful flavouring substance, which cannot be matched by any artificial substitute. The pods are picked by hand, dipped in boiling water, fermented, and then dried, becoming black during the process. The chili pepper, also called in its various forms paprika, pimiento, red pepper, or capsicum, is a valued spice used to flavour the monotonous foods that millions of people eat as their mainstay. It is a small annual with glossy, dark-green leaves, easily raised from seed on rich, well-weeded soil. Its pale-lilac flowers are followed by red or green pointed fruits. These hold a pungent compound, called capsicin, which gives a piquant flavour to any dish.

The 5,000 mile-long mountain chain of the Andes, which falls steeply from heights averaging 12,000 feet to the coastal plain, has its own exceptional flora. In the remote upland forests of Peru grows the quinine tree, *Cinchona ledgeriana*, source of the bark that was for a long time man's only sure defence against malaria. This bark, when first discovered by a Spanish Augustinian missionary, Father Calancha, in about 1633, was already an established Indian remedy. During the mid-1800's, seeds were smuggled out by British and Dutch botanists, and cinchona has since been cultivated as a plantation tree in Indonesia.

In the warmer Andean regions nasturtiums grow wild as annual plants with a short, intense growing season. When rains fall, their large seeds sprout and a trailing shoot extends rapidly over the ground or climbs up neighbouring vegetation. The brilliant orange-red flowers, trumpet-shaped though somewhat lop-sided, soon follow and ripen pods holding seeds that lie dormant until the next rainy season. Calceolarias of many kinds, which originate in the southern Andes, are now grown in many countries for the beauty of their lipped blossoms. They, too, are short-season plants, and in temperate countries are raised in greenhouses, then planted out after the frosts.

In the dry deserts of the central high Andes, which extend from Lake Titicaca south to a latitude of 35 degrees, the plants that survive the worst conditions of drought are the little woolly cactuses. Their dense hairy covering is not, as one might think, a protection against the cold, but a device to cut down water-loss by restricting air flow over the leaf's surface.

Farther south along the Andean chain, on the borders of

southern Chile and the Argentine, where there is more rain and snow, the hardy, bizarre monkey-puzzle tree, or Chile pine, forms extensive forests. A conifer with a geometrical pattern of growth, it has scale-shaped, evergreen leaves that endure for 12 or more years. Some trees bear male catkins, others bear huge female cones, which hold large nutritious seeds that were once a staple food of the local Araucanian Indians. Associated with monkey-puzzles grow the South American beech trees, close allies of the European and North American beeches, with similar smooth, grey bark and small, oval leaves. They are deciduous, fast-growing trees that form large, shady groves on the hillsides. The timber is used in furniture making.

Amidst these tall forest trees fuchsia bushes flourish and bear their quaint drooping blossoms, which have won them a place in gardens throughout most temperate lands. Each flower has an outer ring of coloured sepals, which attract insects to the central tube of interwoven petals that holds the long stamens and pistil.

Plants of the Andes Mountains.

The small cinchona tree (top), which is native to the Peruvian highlands, holds in its bark the drug quinine, an invaluable remedy for malaria.

Left: three beautiful flowers now grown in gardens throughout the world. The shrubby fuchsia (top) bears nodding bell-shaped blooms with reflexed sepals. Calceolarias (middle) are shrubby plants with clusters of bright, purse-shaped blossoms. Nasturtiums (bottom) trail or climb on soft annual stems, carrying brilliant open-mouthed flowers with long spurs.

Above: woolly cactus resists extreme drought on the cold, high Andean summits.

Timber trees of southern Chile. The South American beech (grey), a broad-leaved tree, grows on the Andean foothills. The monkey-puzzle tree (right), a hardy conifer with an oddly geometric branching pattern, bears large cones holding edible seeds.

South American crop plants, now grown everywhere. Tomato (top left) is a scrambling annual that ripens juicy red fruits. Potato (top centre), a perennial, stores food reserves in starchy underground tubers. Tobacco (below left), a leafy annual, contains the soothing drug nicotine in its leaves, which are used for smoking.

Like the tropical rain forest of northern South America, the complex and varied vegetation of the Andes has produced many plants that are now of widespread agricultural importance. Potatoes, for example, grow wild on the lower slopes of the Andes, in a climate with a dry season but no hard frost. They live through the drought by storing nourishment in fleshy underground tubers, and recommence growth from their "eyes," or shoot-buds, when the rains return. The Indians found that potatoes could be cultivated in higher, colder regions provided their tubers were overwintered buried deep below frost level. European explorers introduced this crop to temperate countries, and it became a staple food in many lands.

Tomatoes, too, are native to the lower Andes. They are scrambling annual plants that send fast-growing stems over the undergrowth. Their small, yellow flowers develop into the familiar red, juicy fruits, holding the numerous yellow seeds that ensure the plant's continuance. Although the Indians had long relished these tasty fruits, the tomato was first introduced to Europe as an ornamental plant.

A more vigorous annual climber found in the forests of the Andes, and also in other parts of South America, is the passion flower. Now grown in many parts of the world, the passion flower yields the sweet-tasting passion fruit, which is either eaten raw or crushed to make a delicious, refreshing drink. The passion flower derives its name from the representation of Christ's passion that missionaries saw in its intricate pattern. The projections around the base of the stamens and ovary, for example, were seen to represent Christ's crown of thorns.

One of the most important plants to originate from America is maize, or Indian corn. Although its exact place and time of origin are not known, maize was cultivated by South American Indians, and indeed by all settled Amerindian tribes, long before European explorers arrived. Believed to have arisen as a chance hybrid between two wild grasses, it grows as a sturdy annual that bears feathery male flowers at the tips of six-foot-tall, leafy stems. The female flowers open lower down, in oval clusters that end in tassels of pollen-catching stigmas. The large seed-cobs, each made up of broad, flat, hard, yellow seeds, ripen rapidly. They are used for coarse bread, porridge, breakfast cereals, foods for livestock, and as a base for alcoholic drinks, particularly bourbon whisky.

Tobacco is native to northern South America, Mexico, and the West Indies. It has been cultivated by the Indians for at least a thousand years for the soothing, mildly narcotic nicotine, which it holds in its leaves. A tall annual plant bearing large, oval leaves, it is topped, when mature, by cream-coloured, trumpet-shaped blossoms. The leaves are first withered, then fermented, and finally shredded to provide fragrant tobacco.

The ground cherry, also called the Cape gooseberry because it is widely grown in South Africa, originates in South America. An annual plant with pale-green, heart-shaped leaves, it produces yellow, bell-shaped flowers that are followed by juicy, red berries enclosed in papery, orange-brown capsules. These capsules give it the alternative name of the Chinese lantern.

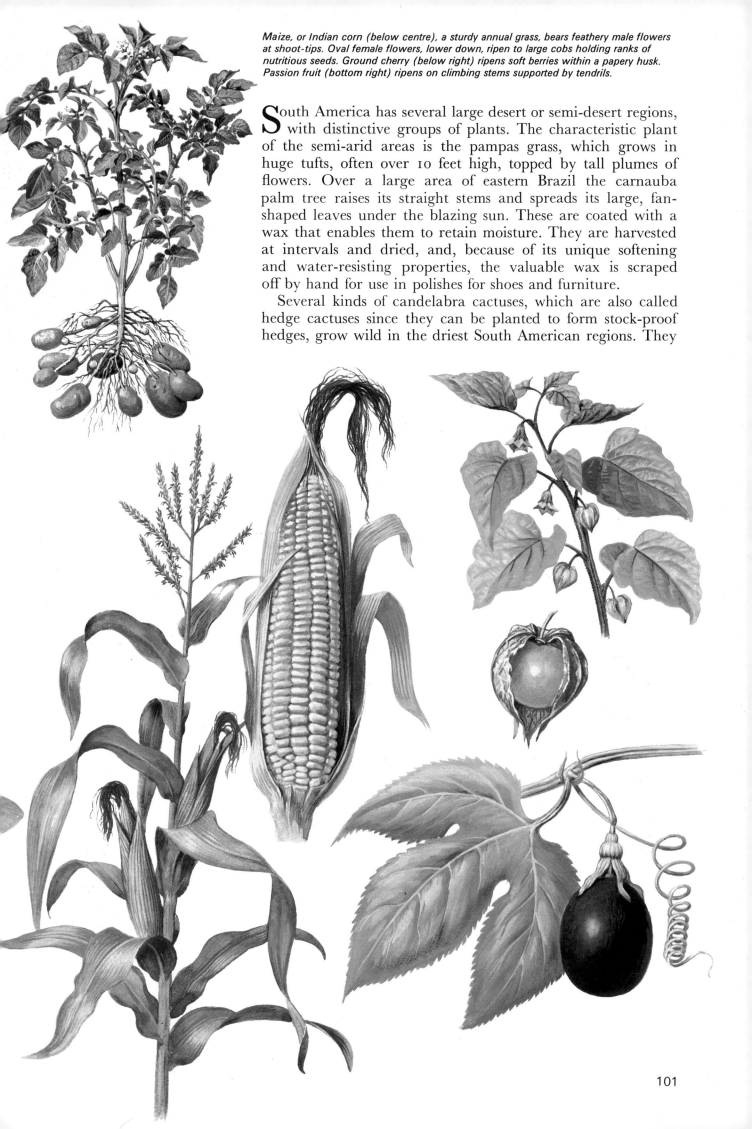

Maize, or Indian corn (below centre), a sturdy annual grass, bears feathery male flowers at shoot-tips. Oval female flowers, lower down, ripen to large cobs holding ranks of nutritious seeds. Ground cherry (below right) ripens soft berries within a papery husk. Passion fruit (bottom right) ripens on climbing stems supported by tendrils.

South America has several large desert or semi-desert regions, with distinctive groups of plants. The characteristic plant of the semi-arid areas is the pampas grass, which grows in huge tufts, often over 10 feet high, topped by tall plumes of flowers. Over a large area of eastern Brazil the carnauba palm tree raises its straight stems and spreads its large, fan-shaped leaves under the blazing sun. These are coated with a wax that enables them to retain moisture. They are harvested at intervals and dried, and, because of its unique softening and water-resisting properties, the valuable wax is scraped off by hand for use in polishes for shoes and furniture.

Several kinds of candelabra cactuses, which are also called hedge cactuses since they can be planted to form stock-proof hedges, grow wild in the driest South American regions. They have fleshy, upright stems that branch repeatedly in a candelabra pattern and may grow 30 feet tall. Each stem has about six sturdy ribs that bear clusters of fierce spines to check browsing animals. There are no leaves, all leaf functions being carried out by the green stems. The white flowers spring directly from the tips of the high stems. In somewhat moister places grows the low Christmas cactus, so named because, when grown as a house plant, it opens its rose-red flowers regularly around Christmas time; it often grows, as an epiphyte, on the branches of forest trees.

In the hot dry zone of south-east Brazil, most plants are adapted to resist drought. Tall carnauba palms (below left) bear fan-shaped leaves coated in wax. The branching candelabra cactuses (background) store water in stout, ridged stems, armed with spines to stop animals browsing. Pampas grasses (below right) grow as dense tufts of narrow-leaved blades, topped by feathery flower-spikes. Christmas cactus (inset) has no true leaves; instead flattened stems do their work, so reducing water-loss.

© Geographical Projects

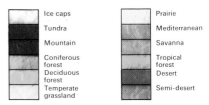

Ice caps	Prairie
Tundra	Mediterranean
Mountain	Savanna
Coniferous forest	Tropical forest
Deciduous forest	Desert
Temperate grassland	Semi-desert

Projection: Bipolar Oblique Conic Conformal
Scale: 1:13,900,000
Miles
0   100   200   300
0   100   200   300   400   500
Kilometres

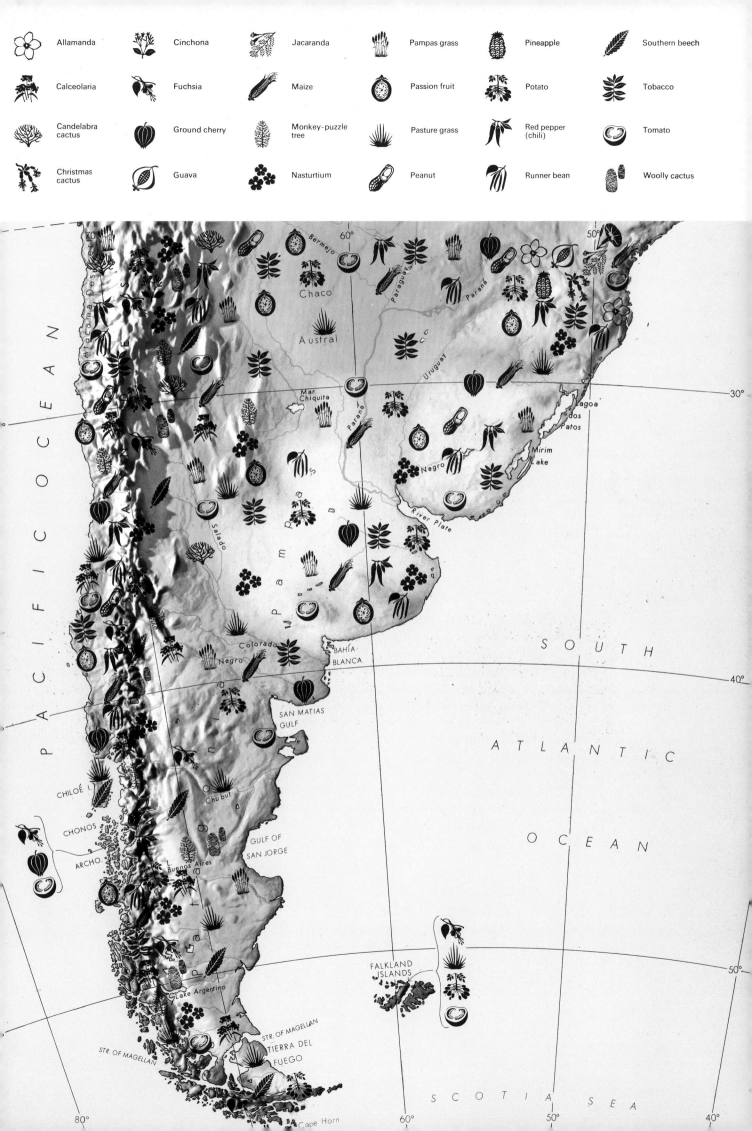

Allamanda	Cinchona	Jacaranda	Pampas grass
Calceolaria	Fuchsia	Maize	Passion fruit
Candelabra cactus	Ground cherry	Monkey-puzzle tree	Pasture grass
Christmas cactus	Guava	Nasturtium	Peanut

Pineapple	Southern beech	
Potato	Tobacco	
Red pepper (chili)	Tomato	
Runner bean	Woolly cactus	

PACIFIC OCEAN

Atacama Desert

Chaco Austral

Bermejo

Paraguay

Paraná

Uruguay

Mar Chiquita

Paraná

Negro

Lagoa dos Patos

Mirim Lake

River Plate

Pampa

Salado

Colorado

Negro

BAHÍA BLANCA

SAN MATIAS GULF

SOUTH ATLANTIC OCEAN

CHILOÉ I.

CHONOS

ARCHO.

Buenos Aires

Chubut

GULF OF SAN JORGE

Lake Argentino

FALKLAND ISLANDS

STR. OF MAGELLAN

STR. OF MAGELLAN

TIERRA DEL FUEGO

SCOTIA SEA

Cape Horn

30°

40°

50°

60°

70°

80°

60°

50°

40°

7 Australasia

Australia's eucalyptus forests and brilliant flowering shrubs. Desert plants that flourish only after rains. Mountain forests of New Zealand: kauri pine, tree fern, and golden-blossomed kowhai.

The continent of Australia forms a great island astride the southern tropic. Although it is surrounded by water, it lies in a tropical zone where the winds carry little moisture inland. As a result the vast "dead heart" of Australia is a torrid sun-baked desert, lacking rainfall and plant life. Around the rim of this desert, on all sides except the south, a scanty supply of rain supports sparse grass—once grazed only by the native kangaroo but now the mainstay of great flocks of Merino sheep and hardy beef cattle, introduced by European settlers.

Close to the eastern seaboard of Australia runs a succession of mountain ridges called the Great Dividing Range. In the south these have a temperate, cloudy climate, with snowy peaks, but farther north the climate becomes warmer. Most of the continent's rain falls on this mountain range, or east of it. Some flows down short, rapid rivers to the east coast, and the rest goes more gradually westwards to reach the sea on north or south coasts, or else disappears in the great inland desert. Northern Australia is influenced by the Asiatic monsoons and has enough warmth and rainfall to support tropical forests, though rains are markedly seasonal. The south-west has a "Mediterranean" climate of hot dry summers and warm moist winters, and supports an evergreen vegetation.

South-eastern Australia, which has a warm temperate climate under which most European crops can be grown, holds a wealth of brilliant flowering shrubs and trees, mostly evergreen. The waratah bush, for example, has erect stems bearing stiff, dark-green leaves, and topped by glowing crimson flower-heads every spring. Its aboriginal name of waratah, preserved in the modern scientific one (*Telopea*), means "seen from afar" in allusion to its vivid colouring. The tall flame tree sheds its dark-green leaves for a brief spell in late spring, just as its scarlet flowers, grouped in intricate clusters, open in a blaze of colour. Another conspicuous tree, the Australian golden

Summer brings a blaze of blossom to shrubs in south-east Australia. Flame trees (top) open scarlet flowers matched by the crimson globes of waratahs (bottom centre). Yellow-orange banksia (left) contrasts with the intense yellow of golden wattle (right). Christmas bells, (bottom right) nod gracefully in clearings.

wattle, displays, every spring, clouds of little, deep-yellow flower-balls over its grey-green foliage. Each flower-ball is a closely packed cluster of many separate flowers, but when these open, their long, bright-yellow stamens obscure the tiny petals at the heart of the flower-group.

The banksias, or tree honeysuckles, grow as long, creeping, woody plants, spreading shrubs, or as tall trees, bearing tough, evergreen leaves. During spring and summer they open conspicuous upright flower-spikes, ranging in colour from yellow through brown to crimson. Each flower-spike, which may be several inches long, consists of densely-packed flowers with an array of protruding styles. They produce abundant nectar and attract many bees—hence the name "honeysuckle." The alternative name banksia commemorates Sir Joseph Banks, the botanist who accompanied Captain Cook on his voyage of exploration in 1770, and found the first specimens at the appropriately named anchorage of Botany Bay.

The most brilliant flowers among the smaller plants of this region are Christmas bells, a relative of the lilies. They open in the southern midsummer, in damp places amid open heathlands. The stiff, dark-green flower-stalk carries at its tip a group of nodding, bell-shaped blossoms, with scarlet tubes ending in a rim of six golden lobes.

The aptly named Snowy Mountains in the east of New South Wales and Victoria carry trees and flowering plants that are adapted to the alpine climate. The snow gum, which

Alpine flowers of the Snowy Mountains in New South Wales. Soft boronia (top left) has fragrant foliage that perfumes the air after each climber's tread. The bright mountain buttercup (lower left) and alpine bluebell (inset), come up through melting snow on gravel beds. Rugged snow gum (above), hardiest of the eucalyptus tribe, grows at higher levels than any other Australian tree.

Remarkable trees of Queensland forests.
Bunya pine (black outline) is a conifer
with a geometrical pattern of branching
and stiff, pointed, evergreen leaves.
Barrel tree (above) stores water through
the dry season in its swollen trunk.
Moreton Bay chestnut (lower right)
bears large compound leaves and
drooping pods holding nutritious nuts.
Inset above: two striking flowers from
forest clearings; the purplish-blue fringe
lily, and the pale-yellow flannel flower.

grows here, is a typical member of the eucalypts, or gum trees.
Eucalypts, native only to Australia, are evergreen, broad-leaved
trees with two types of foliage. In youth their leaves are broad
and clasp the stem; later they open narrow, stalked, adult
leaves that hang vertically, letting the sun's rays filter through
the foliage. The hardiest of this tribe, snow gum, grows amid
rocks and screes up to the limit of vegetation.

The mountain buttercup, which has golden, bowl-shaped
blossoms carried above pale-green foliage, is one of many
alpine plants that have only a short growing season. As soon as
the snow melts, it sends up shoots from its stout rootstock,
flowers, and sets seeds before winter's cold returns. The alpine
bluebell, with slender hairy leaves that lose little moisture,
thrives in dry places and can succeed even when rooted only in
fine crevices in the rocks. Better soils are often covered by the
trailing stems of the boronias, woody plants bearing evergreen
leaves, and abundant pale-pink, star-shaped flowers.

Farther north, on the lower hills and coastal plain of Queensland, the sub-tropical climate supports a rich rain forest
holding many evergreen and a few deciduous trees. The bunya
pine, known as bunya-bunya to the aborigines who gather
edible seeds from its fallen cones, is a native conifer related
to the monkey-puzzle tree of South America.

Another tree valued by the aborigines for its nutritious seeds
is the Moreton Bay chestnut, a tall evergreen with feathery
compound leaves. Its timber, marketed as black bean, is an

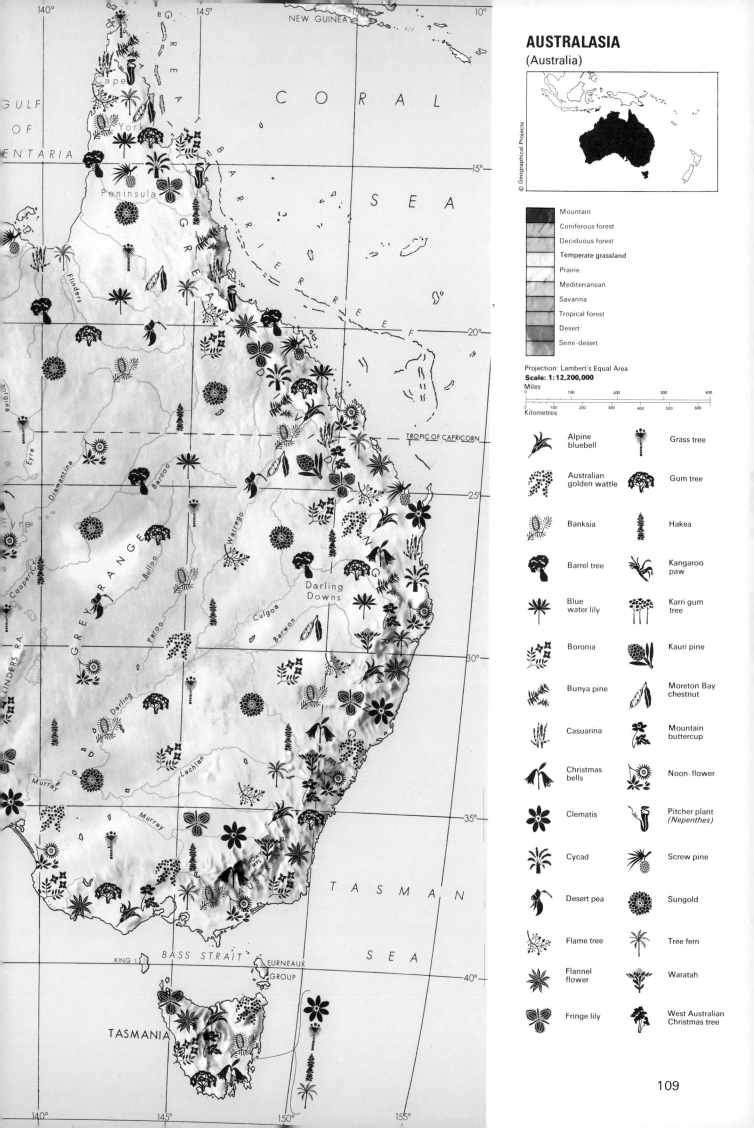

Mountain
Coniferous forest
Deciduous forest
Temperate grassland
Prairie
Mediterranean
Savanna
Tropical forest
Desert
Semi-desert

Projection: Lambert's Equal Area
Scale: 1:12,200,000

Miles
0   100   200   300   400
0   100   200   300   400   500   600
Kilometres

Alpine bluebell		Grass tree	
Australian golden wattle		Gum tree	
Banksia		Hakea	
Barrel tree		Kangaroo paw	
Blue water lily		Karri gum tree	
Boronia		Kauri pine	
Bunya pine		Moreton Bay chestnut	
Casuarina		Mountain buttercup	
Christmas bells		Noon-flower	
Clematis		Pitcher plant (Nepenthes)	
Cycad		Screw pine	
Desert pea		Sungold	
Flame tree		Tree fern	
Flannel flower		Waratah	
Fringe lily		West Australian Christmas tree	

Map labels:

NEW GUINEA

CORAL SEA

GULF OF CARPENTARIA

Cape York Peninsula

GREAT BARRIER REEF

Flinders

TROPIC OF CAPRICORN

Eyre

Diamantina

Cooper's Cr

Barcoo

Warrego

GREY RANGE

Bulloo

Paroo

FLINDERS RA.

Darling

Culgoa

Barwon

Darling Downs

GREAT DIVIDING RANGE

Lachlan

Murray

Murray

Snowy Mts

AUSTRALIAN ALPS

TASMAN SEA

BASS STRAIT

KING I.

FURNEAUX GROUP

TASMANIA

109

outstandingly beautiful wood, boldly patterned in rich brown and black, and with an intricate and varied grain.

The barrel, or bottle, tree is so-called because of its great swollen trunk, which has the same function as a man-made barrel—to store water. The trunk of a 100-foot-tall tree is often 10 feet in diameter, and in dry seasons the aborigines tap such trunks in order to drink the sap.

On the forest floor, many low, shade-tolerant plants display bright flowers to attract insects. One of these, the daisy-shaped flannel flower, gets its name from the coarse, soft texture of its pale cream, oblong petals. The fringe lily, loveliest of the Queensland wild flowers, bears exquisitely shaped blossoms of an intense purplish-blue shade on slender stalks amid grass-like foliage. Each petal has a delicate fringe of hairs, the movement of which helps pollinating insects to find the flower.

In northern Australia, the combination of seasonal heavy rainfall and brilliant tropical sunshine over most of the year obliges both plants and trees to assume exceptional forms and life cycles. The tough-timbered casuarina, or she-oak tree, which grows along streamsides and along sea-beaches, bears bunches of exceptionally fine twigs. The leaves are reduced to scales, which lessens water-loss and enables the she-oak to survive long droughts.

By contrast, the little sungolds, or paper-daisies, are short-lived annuals that pass the hot dry summer as seeds. When the rains come, these sprout and grow rapidly into shoots that bear

After the seasonal rains this creek on the desert fringes of Australia's Northern Territory carries water lilies floating on its surface. Drought-resistant casuarina trees wave their feathery foliage overhead. Encouraged by moisture, bright flowers open on sandbanks; here are scarlet desert pea, everlasting sungold, and star-shaped noon-flower.

110

The tallest tree of Western Australia's forests is the magnificent karri gum (background), a eucalyptus with blue-green foliage and flaking bark. In drier country the grass-tree (above) opens knob-shaped flower heads above a tuft of slender leaves. West Australian Christmas tree (above right) becomes a blaze of gold in midsummer. Shown immediately above are lantern hakea and the quaint kangaroo-paw flower.

small, green leaves and yellow flower-heads. The centre of each head consists of golden flowers, around which radiates a golden crown of papery flower-like bracts. Sungolds are often gathered as everlasting flowers for decoration.

The blue, or giant, water lily can endure dry spells as a fleshy rootstock in the mud of a dry creek. When the water returns, it sends up long stalks to float its huge, heart-shaped leaves on the surface. It opens mauve, star-shaped flowers, up to a foot across, with many radiating petals and a ball of golden stamens.

The quaint desert pea survives on the arid sands of central Australia by tapping the water, brought by occasional rain-storms, that remains trapped in the lower soil. Its grey-green, compound leaves bear silky hairs that cut down water-loss, and its brilliant scarlet flowers attract insects over a long dis-tance. Noon-flowers store water from infrequent rains in their very thick, fleshy stems and leaves. Their abundant flowers are daisy-shaped, with white centres and radiating crimson petals. They open fully only at mid-day, which explains the name "noon-flower."

South-west Australia receives ample rain during the southern winter, around July, but is hot and dry for the rest of the year. Here grow forests of karri gum tree, one of the grandest eucalypts. Its smooth-barked, yellowish-white trunk, with blue-grey patches, may scale 30 feet around, and soar up-wards for 250 feet. Karri timber is red in colour, very strong, hard, and heavy. Its forests are a valued economic resource,

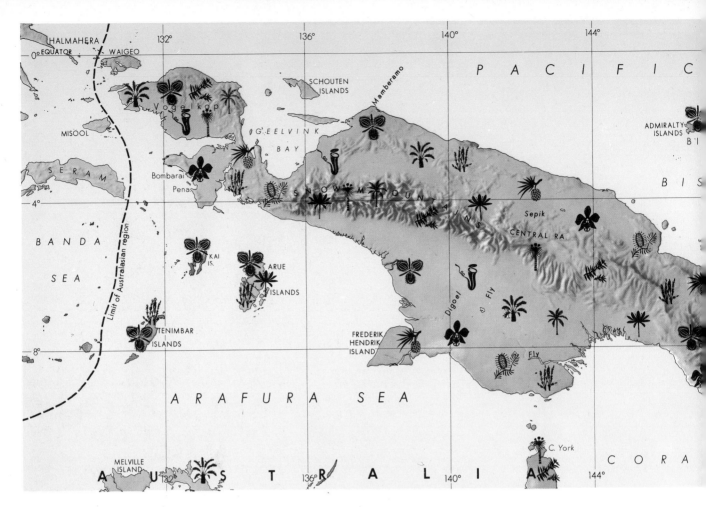

AUSTRALASIA
(New Guinea)

■	Mountain
▨	Savanna
▨	Tropical forest

Projection: Mercator
Scale: 1:11,020,000

Miles
0   100   200   300

Kilometres
0   100   200   300   400

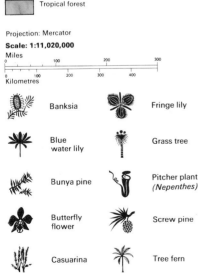

Banksia	Fringe lily
Blue water lily	Grass tree
Bunya pine	Pitcher plant (Nepenthes)
Butterfly flower	Screw pine
Casuarina	Tree fern
Cycad	

since karri is exported for engineering and shipbuilding work.

The grass trees that are found here and also in other parts of Australia grow as single, upright stems bearing a dense clothing of fine, grass-like foliage. As the older blades mature and die, others appear higher up. The leaf bases remain and can be counted, and from the known rate of leaf replacement it has been calculated that some grass trees are over 4,000 years old. Grass trees are also called blackboys because sometimes bush fires char their stems, turning them black yet rarely killing the tree. According to species each tree produces one or several flower-heads, each borne on a long stalk above the grass tuft.

A tall shrub adapted to grow under the "Mediterranean" climatic conditions of south-west Australia is the spectacular lantern hakea, so called because its tough, grey-green foliage has bright-orange zones that glow in the sun. All hakeas bear showy flowers with long protruding styles. A plant native to Western Australia, the aptly-named kangaroo paw, bears furry flower stalks and hairy flowers. Colours vary; in the red-and-green kangaroo paw the flower-stalk is crimson and the curved, strap-shaped flowers are pale green.

In December, the West Australian Christmas tree breaks into a vivid outburst of colour, with brilliant orange blossoms hiding its needle-shaped leaves. Though it becomes a woody tree up to 40 feet high, it can grow only as a semi-parasite. Below ground, its roots tap those of banksia bushes, and even grasses, to gain water and nutrients.

New Guinea, a large island near the equator, with a long mountainous spine, has a tropical climate with high rainfall. Its vast range of plant life shows links with Australia to the

In New Guinea's mountain jungles, primitive trees thrive beside highly evolved flowering plants. The cycad (centre) resembles a palm but is halfway between a fern and a flowering plant. Screw pine (right) has leaves in spirals and fruits like pineapples. Butterfly flower (left) mimics the pollinating butterflies it attracts. The pitcher plant beneath traps insects in highly modified leaves.

south and Asia to the north. A conspicuous group here are the cycads, or zamias, palm-like plants and trees that were a dominant feature of plant life about 200 million years ago. Each cycad has a single shoot that bears at its tip a tuft of enormous, feathery leaves, often three feet long. Cycads are long-lived; fresh leaves sprout only at intervals of a year or so, and counts of leaf-bases have suggested ages of 14,000 years!

Another outstanding group of New Guinea trees is that of the screw pines, also called screw palms and *Pandanus* trees. They get their common names from their palm-like appearance and from the spiral arrangement of the seeds on the huge fruits, which resemble pineapples. Many screw pines grow in marshy places, and are supported on stilt roots.

The butterfly flower, or moth orchid, is one of many beautiful orchids that thrive in the New Guinea rain forests. It is an epiphyte that grows on tree bark, but has no bulb, just a short, woody stem bearing oval, dark-green fleshy leaves. Its flower-spike carries many dainty white blossoms, with orange lower petals, that nod on long stalks like flying butterflies.

The New Guinea pitcher plant, *Nepenthes*, usually grows on bark, on fallen logs, or in similar situations, such as the peaty jungle floor, where it cannot readily draw nutrients from the mineral soil. It gains additional nourishment by trapping and digesting insects in its modified leaves. Crawling insects enter the "pitcher" easily but cannot escape because of its incurved rim. Eventually they fall into a pool of liquid held at its base,

Trees, climbers, and flowers of New Zealand's lowland forests. Tall kauri pines (right) tower above graceful tree ferns (left). Rata vines with bright scarlet blossoms (centre) scramble over undershrubs. Bottom right: exquisite flowers of bush clematis, and waving spikes of toe-toe grass.

AUSTRALASIA
(New Zealand)

© Geographical Projects

Legend (vegetation types):
- Mountain
- Coniferous forest
- Deciduous forest
- Temperate grassland
- Prairie

Projection: Conic
Scale: 1 : 5,900,000

Miles
0   50   100   150
0   50   100   150   200   250   300
Kilometres

Plant symbols:
- Alpine bluebell
- Cabbage tree
- Clematis
- Kauri pine
- Koromiko
- Kowhai
- Mountain buttercup
- Rata
- Tea-tree
- Toe-toe grass
- Tree-daisy
- Tree fern

THREE KINGS ISLANDS

NORTH ISLAND

GREAT BARRIER ISLAND

HAURAKI GULF

BAY OF PLENTY

Waikato

Taupo

MT. EGMONT

HAWKE BAY

Wanganui

Rangitiki

TASMAN

SEA

TASMAN BAY

COOK STRAIT

SOUTH ISLAND

Grey

Banks Pena.

CANTERBURY BIGHT

CANTERBURY Plains

Rangitata

Clutha

Oreti

FOVEAUX STRAIT

STEWART ISLAND

SNARES IS.

PACIFIC

OCEAN

BOUNTY IS.

36°
40°
44°
48°

166°   170°   174°   178°

and drown. The leaf then absorbs the nutrients dissolved from their decaying bodies. The flowers, borne on shoots quite distinct from the pitchers, are small and white.

New Zealand's two islands, North Island and South Island lie close together in the South Pacific Ocean, and their lowlands have a climate of warm summers and mild winters with ample year-round rainfall. Most trees and plants are evergreens, adapted to grow over most of the year, with only a brief winter resting spell. But growth is strictly seasonal on the 8,000-foot range of the New Zealand Alps, which run for 350 miles down the western side of South Island. Here there are snow-capped peaks and great glaciers, and only alpine plants, which grow actively only in summer, can survive.

The kauri pine forms great forests of tall timber trees over the warm northern lowlands of North Island. Though it is a conifer, it differs from the Northern Hemisphere pines in having broad leaves rather than needles. The male cones are green and oblong and the round-topped, blue female cones have only one seed below each scale, whereas northern pines have two. Kauri can grow 150 feet tall, with a stem 70 feet around, and to an estimated age of 4,000 years. A valuable resin, called kauri gum, runs through the tree and oozes from injured stems. It is used for making paints, varnishes, and linoleum.

Tree ferns, which grow throughout the New Zealand forests, have a structure and life cycle like that of commoner kinds of ferns. Instead of remaining short as in common ferns, the main stem of the tree fern grows steadily taller, though not stouter, and becomes woody. Like cycads, tree ferns are survivors of the dominant vegetation of 200 million years ago. New Zealand's commonest tree fern, *Dicksonia antarctica,* may develop a trunk 20 feet tall, with fronds six feet long waving above this. Aerial roots often sprout from its growing point and trail down to the ground.

The brilliantly flowered rata vine that trails over the undergrowth and scrambles up shrubs into the tree crowns is one of several ratas native to New Zealand, and found nowhere else. Ratas are woody plants with evergreen, glossy, oval leaves and

*Striking shrubs and trees native to
New Zealand.*

*Tea-tree (top left) with waxy flowers and
fine, fragrant foliage, and koromiko, a
Hebe with graceful flower-spikes and
glossy, evergreen leaves.*

*The cabbage tree (centre) is grown in
many subtropical gardens for its
palm-like form. Tree-daisy (above) has
glossy, salt-resistant foliage and starry
flowers.*

*The brilliant kowhai (left), New
Zealand's national flower, displays
yellow blossoms on leafless stems.*

bright summer flowers, red or white in colour. Each blossom has a golden central disc, small petals, and a mop-head of long red or white stamens tipped with golden anthers. Another beautiful forest scrambler is the bush clematis, or puawhanganga, one of several kinds that climb by means of leaf stalks modified to form strong, twining tendrils. It bears large, fragrant, white flowers, up to four inches across, which are followed by feathery seed-heads. Each of its many seeds is carried away on the wind, suspended from a plume of hairs. The seedlings climb up undergrowth and eventually become tough, woody vines, up to 6o feet long.

Outside the forest shades much open country carries the toe-toe, or tussock, grass, a tall perennial kind that bears magnificent white, plume-shaped flower-heads. A taller plant that springs up amid the tussocks is the cabbage tree, so called because early settlers gathered its tender central shoot and cooked it for eating. Also called cordyline, it is grown today as a decorative tree in many countries with a mild climate, because of its attractive palm-like form.

The kowhai, which like many New Zealand plants retains its original Maori name, is a low bush that bears bright-yellow, sweet-pea-shaped flowers. These are so conspicuous that the kowhai has been adopted as the country's national flower. Its long leaves are compound, with many paired leaflets, and the fruit is a dry seed-pod. Another distinctive New Zealand shrub is the tea-tree, or manuka, which carries beautiful blossoms along slender twigs bearing narrow leaves. The plant is named for the aromatic fragrance of these leaves. In the wild race, the five-petalled flowers are white with dark centres; under cultivation pink and crimson strains, some with double flowers, have been developed.

Two groups of low evergreen shrubs that grow, in one variety or another, all over New Zealand, have been introduced to most temperate countries and planted widely for their high decorative value. The *Olearias*, or tree-daisies, have leathery, dark-green leaves, carried on spreading, woody twigs. Their fragrant, daisy-shaped flowers, with white ray florets and golden centres, open in abundant clusters each summer and are followed by tufts of hairy seeds. The *Hebe* genus, which includes the koromiko and the New Zealand lilac, consists of low, much-branched shrubs with slender, evergreen, glossy-surfaced leaves set in pairs. Their long, narrow flower-spikes carry scores of small, white, mauve or blue blossoms that open profusely all summer through.

8 Plants to New Lands

Once man had discovered how to cultivate crop plants he began to take them to fresh places, by carrying seeds, bulbs, or cuttings to new ground. For thousands of years this was a gradual process, for overland transport was slow. Yet it resulted in many useful plants from Asia, such as wheat, being introduced to most parts of Europe, while the American Indians carried their own staple grain crop, maize, to many regions of North, Central, and South America.

The rapid development of sea exploration, from the 1400's onwards, enabled men to carry living plants over thousands of miles of seaways in a short space of time. One of the explorers' main objects was to find fresh places for settlement, where they could build homesteads, grow the same crops, and tend the same animals as they had known in their own countries. In addition there was the hope that newly discovered countries might hold strange plants that could be brought back to the home country, to be grown as a new food source, or perhaps as spices to enliven a dull everyday diet.

As the new colonists and their plantations spread in different tropical lands, settlers started to carry crop plants, which would not grow in the colder temperate countries, from one warm continent to another. Many of these introductions took place in the course of general trade, and were not recorded as remarkable, or specially planned events.

Other transplantations, however, were deliberately planned. In 1787 the British government, on the advice of a famous botanist and explorer, Sir Joseph Banks, sent the ship *Bounty* to the island of Tahiti in the South Pacific to procure breadfruit plants for cultivation in Jamaica. On the return voyage, the crew mutinied against their commander, Captain Bligh, and set him adrift in an open boat with a few loyal seamen. Finally, in 1793, Bligh succeeded in landing a stock of Tahitian breadfruit in the West Indies, from a fresh ship.

One of the earliest trans-ocean transplants was sugar cane. Originally an Indonesian plant, it was carried through India

Colonists settling in fresh lands always carry stocks of their familiar food plants. Here a Pilgrim Father from England strides ashore on the east coast of North America, carrying his group's most treasured possession—seed wheat. This, they believe, will ensure their survival. However strange their new homeland, they can always grow their own wheat.

and Arabia to the Mediterranean region, where it was cultivated in the 700's. Later it was taken from Spain to the West Indies by Columbus on his second voyage, in 1493, at the command of King Ferdinand and Queen Isabella. Around 1600 sugar cane was carried by Portuguese colonists to southern Africa, and eventually, in about 1800, to Queensland in Australia. Sugar cultivation expanded rapidly in the Caribbean. Thousands of African slaves worked on the European-owned plantations producing sugar for shipment to Europe and North America.

The orange tree, which originated in China, and was taken very early on in the Christian era to Mediterranean shores, was carried across the Atlantic Ocean by Spanish navigators, from 1500 onwards. Around 1600, Portuguese navigators encountered it in the Far East, and took it to southern Africa during their homeward voyages. Wheat, which had been carried from its homeland in south-west Asia to western Europe by prehistoric cultivators, was taken by Portuguese settlers to southern Africa around 1500, and to Brazil in about 1550. Soon after the year 1600, English settlers in Virginia and Massachusetts succeeded in growing it on the North American continent, where it has now become the leading grain crop of the inland prairies. Coffee was another significant introduction from the Mediterranean region to the New World. Strains that had originated in Arabia and Ethiopia were taken to Brazil in about 1650, and to the West Indies around 1700.

The return traffic from South America to Europe began equally early, around 1500. Potatoes, which the Spanish conquistadores found being cultivated by Indians on the high Andes of Peru, were carried overland across the Isthmus of Panama and thence to Europe. Later they were taken east by the Dutch to the East Indies and, surprisingly, back across the Atlantic by Irish immigrants to North America, where they are still sometimes called "Irish" potatoes. Maize, the leading grain crop of the Incas, took a similar course, though its cultivation was already widely spread throughout both North and South America before Europeans arrived.

The American Indians introduced the European colonists to tobacco, and smoking became so popular that this American plant was soon carried to many Old World countries where it is widely grown today, notably the Balkans, Turkey, and South Africa. Pineapples were also taken, in the 1500's, from their homeland in Brazil to Spain, Portugal, West Africa, India, and the East Indies, but their introductions to Hawaii and to Queensland in Australia, both leading centres of cultivation today, did not occur until about 1800.

In the course of trade between various tropical colonies, Portuguese navigators carried the cassava, or tapioca plant first to West Africa and later around the Cape of Good Hope to the East Indies. In both these regions its cultivation spread from European settlements to peasant farms and it soon ranked as a major food resource. Cocoa was discovered, as an established Indian drink, by Columbus, but his attempt to cultivate the tree that produces it, under the drier climate of Spain in 1501, proved a failure. Later, around 1600, it was taken to

Above: an American Indian chief offers a gift of fruit and potatoes to a Spanish explorer, who will take them back to Europe and attempt their cultivation there. Though most tropical fruits failed, potatoes became a staple food crop in temperate lands.

Below: Captain Bligh of the Bounty *instructs a sailor to dig up breadfruit plants in Tahiti. They are to be transplanted from the Pacific to the British West Indies, as a new source of food for the colonists and their slaves.*

West Africa, which now supplies the bulk of the world's needs.

Tomatoes, taken from South America to Europe in the late 1500's, were at first regarded as ornamental plants, bearing the quaint name of "love apple." Later, when their value as a salad and cooking fruit was better appreciated, they were taken to all countries where Europeans settled.

The banana, native to India and the East Indies, provides a remarkable example of the way in which the restless European colonizers enriched the diet of the tropical peoples in the lands where they settled. Around 1500, returning Portuguese voyagers carried this easily cultivated plant to south-east Africa, West Africa, and the Canary Islands. Thence it was taken across the Atlantic to the West Indies and South America, where today it is grown for export to Europe and North America.

Food plants were naturally the first to be transplanted, but decorative flowering plants soon followed. The larger-flowered kinds of gladiolus grow only in South Africa, but from 1800 onwards they were quickly spread, by means of their easily transported dry corms, to Europe, North and South America, Far East, and even to Australasia. The chrysanthemum, developed by Japanese gardeners, was also distributed to gardens in temperate and subtropical zones.

The cinchona plant, which yields the anti-malarial drug quinine, is native only to a limited region in the high Peruvian Andes. The uncertainty of its supply, and its high cost, led the British and Dutch colonial authorities to smuggle out seeds, in 1860, in order to establish plantations in Sri Lanka and Java. For the same reasons, the British introduced the Pará rubber tree from its Brazilian homeland to Sri Lanka and Malaysia. In 1876, Sir Henry Wickham brought seeds from the Amazon Basin to Kew Gardens in Surrey, and the following year the resulting seedlings were carried to eastern tropical lands with a climate suitable for their growth.

Timber trees were the last great group of plants to attract and reward keen cultivators seeking to improve national resources. The Douglas fir, native to the temperate rain forests of British Columbia and Oregon, was sent as seed by the botanical explorer, David Douglas, to England in 1827. It was soon being widely planted in European forests, and a further introduction, to Australia and New Zealand around 1900, proved equally fruitful. Monterey pine, native only to a small windswept peninsula in southern California, was introduced on a major scale, around 1900, to many countries with subtropical climates. Eucalyptus trees, native only to Australia, were also spread by enterprising foresters, around the year 1900, to a wide range of subtropical lands.

Today there seems little prospect of new plants, of value for large-scale cultivation, being found worth transplanting to new lands. But botanists, farmers, and foresters are constantly aiming to improve all the plants grown commercially, and when a new strain is found and proved it is quickly carried to fresh countries where it is likely to thrive. Plant movement across national frontiers is now controlled by quarantine laws, to ensure that only healthy stocks or seeds are introduced.

PLANTS SPREAD BY MAN

These maps show examples of plants that have been taken overseas and cultivated successfully in different parts of the world. The routes shown are generalized and are, in most cases, dated to the nearest half-century. Where firm dates are known these are used. The maps are arranged across the two pages in chronological order of the earliest-known passage of each plant.

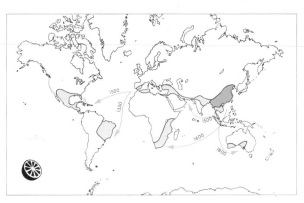

1. Orange (*Citrus sinensis*)

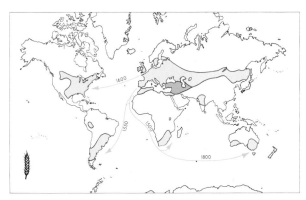

4. Wheat (*Triticum aestivum*)

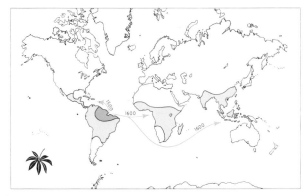

5. Cassava (*Manihot utilissima*)

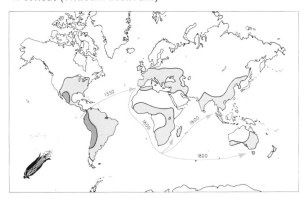

8. Maize (*Zea mays*)

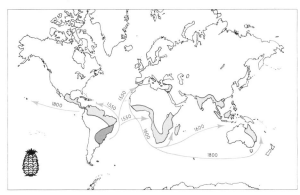

9. Pineapple (*Ananas comosus*)

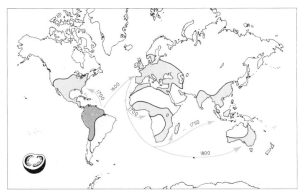

12. Tomato (*Lycopersicon esculentum*)

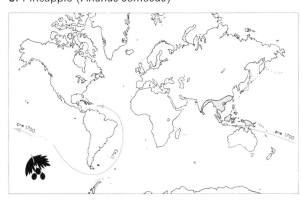

13. Breadfruit (*Artocarpus communis*)

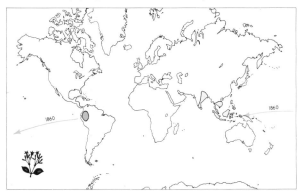

16. Cinchona (*Cinchona ledgeriana*)

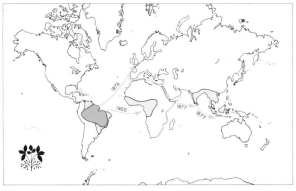

17. Rubber (*Hevea brasiliensis*)

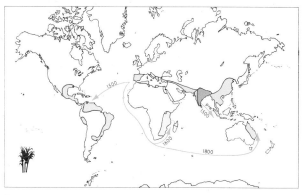

2. Sugar cane (*Saccharum officinarum*)

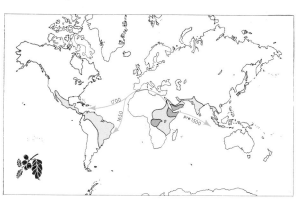

3. Coffee (*Coffea arabica*)

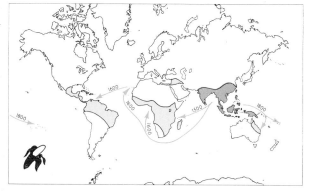

6. Banana (*Musa sapientum*)

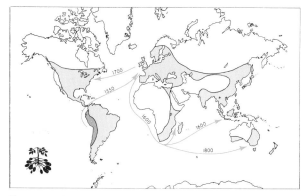

7. Potato (*Solanum tuberosum*)

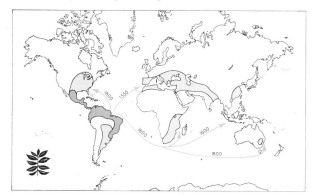

10. Tobacco (*Nicotiana tabacum*)

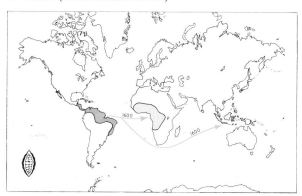

11. Cocoa (*Theobroma cacao*)

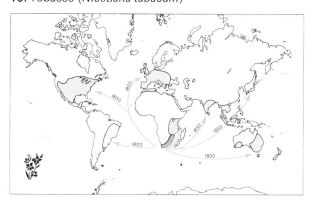

14. Gladiolus (*Gladiolus* spp.)

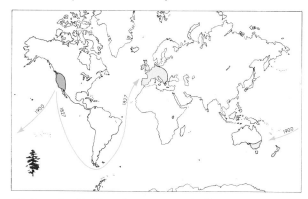

15. Douglas fir (*Pseudotsuga menziesii*)

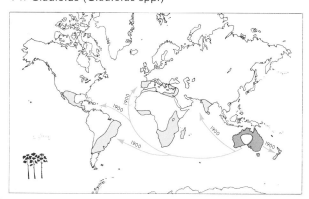

18. Eucalyptus (*Eucalyptus* spp.)

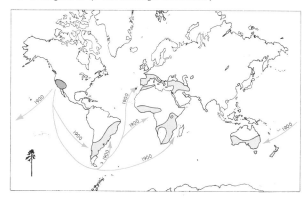

19. Monterey pine (*Pinus radiata*)

Scientific Names

Acidanthera	*Acidanthera bicolor*
African violet	*Saintpaulia ionanthe*
Agave	*Agave sisalana*
Allamanda	*Allamanda cathartica*
Aloe	*Aloe bainesii*
Alpine bluebell	*Wahlenbergia stricta*
Aspen	*Populus tremuloides*
Australian golden wattle	*Acacia pycnantha*
Avocado pear	*Persea americana*
Bald cypress	*Taxodium distichum*
Bamboo	*Dendrocalamus giganteus*
Banana	*Musa sapientium*
Banksia	*Banksia marginata*
Banyan tree	*Ficus bengalensis*
Baobab	*Adansonia digitata*
Barley	*Hordeum vulgare*
Barrel tree	*Brachychiton rupestre*
Beech	*Fagus sylvatica*
Beetroot	*Beta vulgaris*
Bilberry	*Vaccinium myrtillus*
Birch	*Betula pendula*
Blue water lily	*Nymphaea gigantea*
Bluebell	*Endymion non-scripta*
Blueberry	*Vaccinium corymbosum*
Blueblossom	*Ceanothus thyrsiflorus*
Boronia	*Boronia mollis*
Brazil nut	*Bertholletia excelsa*
Breadfruit	*Artocarpus communis*
Broad bean	*Vicia faba*
Bunya pine	*Araucaria bidwilli*
Bush clematis	*Clematis paniculata*
Buttercup	*Ranunculus acris*
Butterfly flower	*Phalaenopsis amabilis*
Cabbage	*Brassica oleracea*
Cabbage tree	*Cordyline australis*
Calceolaria	*Calceolaria integrifolia*
Californian redwood	*Sequoia sempervirens*
Canada lily	*Lilium canadense*
Candelabra cactus	*Cereus hexagonus*
Canna	*Canna indica*
Carnauba palm tree	*Copernicia cerifera*
Carrion flower	*Stapelia variegata*
Cassava	*Manihot utilissima*
Casuarina	*Casuarina equisitifolia*
Ceriman	*Monstera deliciosa*
Cherry laurel	*Prunus laurocerasus*
Chicory	*Cichorium intybus*
Christmas bells	*Blandfordia nobilis*
Christmas cactus	*Schlumbergera truncata*
Chrysanthemum	*Chrysanthemum indicum*
Cinchona	*Cinchona ledgeriana*
Clivia	*Clivia miniata*
Cocksfoot grass	*Dactylis glomerata*
Cocoa	*Theobroma cacao*
Coconut palm	*Cocos nucifera*
Coffee	*Coffea arabica*
Common oak	*Quercus pedunculata*
Cork oak	*Quercus suber*
Cotton	*Gossypium hirsutum*
Cotton grass	*Eriophorum vaginatum*
Cowpea	*Vigna unguiculata*
Cranberry	*Vaccinium macrocarpon*
Crimson clover	*Trifolium incarnatum*
Crocus	*Crocus vernus*
Crown of thorns	*Euphorbia splendens*
Cycad	*Cycas media*
Dahlia	*Dahlia rosea*
Date palm	*Phoenix dactylifera*
Dendrobium orchid	*Dendrobium nobile*
Desert pea	*Clianthus formosus*
Douglas fir	*Pseudotsuga menziesii*
Doum palm	*Hyphaene theobaica*
Dracaena	*Dracaena spp.*
Dryas plant	*Dryas octopetala*
Dwarf willow	*Salix repens*
Ebony	*Diospyros mespiliformis*
Edelweiss	*Leontopodium alpinum*
Egyptian paper reed	*Cyperus papyrus*
Elephant grass	*Pennisetum villosum*
Evening primrose	*Oenothera biennis*
Evergreen oak	*Quercus ilex*
Fig	*Ficus carica*
Flag iris	*Iris pseudacorus*
Flame tree	*Brachychiton acerifolium*
Flamingo flower	*Anthurium scherzerianum*
Flannel flower	*Actinotis helianthi*
Flax	*Linum usitatissimum*
Flowering dogwood	*Cornus florida*
Foxglove	*Digitalis purpurea*

Fringe lily	*Thysanotus tuberosus*
Fuchsia	*Fuchsia magellanica*
Gentian	*Gentiana kochiana*
Giant Amazon water lily	*Victoria cruziana*
Giant sequoia	*Sequoiadendron giganteum*
Gladiolus	*Gladiolus nanus*
Glasswort	*Salicornia europaea*
Gourd	*Lagenaria siceraria*
Grass tree	*Kingia australis*
Ground cherry	*Physalis pruinosa*
Guava	*Psidium guajava*
Guernsey lily	*Nerine sarniensis*
Gum arabic	*Acacia senegal*
Gum tree	*Eucalyptus saligna*
Haller's pulsatilla	*Pulsatilla halleri*
Hawthorn	*Crataegus monogyna*
Hazel	*Corylus avellana*
Heather	*Calluna vulgaris*
Hemlock tree	*Tsuga canadensis*
Hemlock plant	*Conium maculatum*
Hemp	*Cannabis sativa*
Hibiscus	*Hibiscus rosa-sinensis*
Himalayan cedar	*Cedrus deodara*
Himalayan primula	*Primula denticulata*
Holly	*Ilex aquifolium*
Honey locust	*Gleditsia texana*
Hop	*Humulus lupus*
Hyacinth	*Hyacinthus orientalis*
Ivy	*Hedera helix*
Jacaranda	*Jacaranda acutifolia*
Jamaica thatchpalm	*Thrinax parviflora*
Japanese cedar	*Cryptomeria japonica*
Joshua-tree	*Yucca brevifolia*
Juniper	*Juniperus communis*
Jute	*Corchorus capsularis*
Kangaroo paw	*Anigosanthus manglesii*
Karri gum tree	*Eucalyptus diversicolor*
Kauri pine	*Agathis excelsa*
Kentucky bluegrass	*Poa pratensis*
Koromiko	*Hebe stricta*
Kowhai	*Sophora microphylla*
Lantern hakea	*Hakea victoriae*
Larch	*Larix decidua*
Longleaf pine	*Pinus palustris*
Lotus	*Nelumbo nucifera*
Madrone	*Arbutus menziesii*
Mahogany	*Swietenia macrophylla*
Maidenhair tree	*Ginkgo biloba*
Maize	*Zea mays*
Mango	*Mangifera indica*
Mescal button cactus	*Lophophora williamsii*
Mesembryanthemum	*Mesembryanthemum criniflorum*
Mesquite	*Prosopis juliflora*
Millet	*Sorghum vulgare*
Mistletoe	*Viscum album*
Monkey-puzzle tree	*Araucaria araucana*
Monkshood	*Aconitum napellus*
Moreton Bay chestnut	*Castanospermum australe*
Morning glory	*Ipomoea tricolor*
Moroccan broom	*Genista cinerea*
Mountain buttercup	*Ranunculus graniticola*
Mulberry	*Morus nigra*
Mushroom	*Agaricus campestris*
Nasturtium	*Tropaeolum majus*
Noon-flower	*Disphyma australis*
Nutmeg	*Myrica fragrans*
Oak	*Quercus robur*
Oat	*Avena sativa*
Oil palm	*Elaeis guineensis*
Okra	*Hibiscus esculentus*
Olive	*Olea europaea*
Onion	*Allium cepa*
Opium poppy	*Papaver somniferum*
Orange	*Citrus sinensis*
Pampas grass	*Cortaderia selloana*
Papaya	*Carica papaya*
Pará rubber tree	*Hevea brasiliensis*
Passion fruit	*Passiflora edulis*
Pasture grass	*Festuca ovina*
Peach	*Prunus persica*
Peanut	*Arachis hypogaea*
Pecan	*Carya illinoensis*
Pelargonium	*Pelargonium inquinans*

Pepper	*Piper nigrum*
Persimmon	*Diospyros virginiana*
Petunia	*Petunia hybrida*
Pickerel weed	*Pontederia cordata*
Pine	*Pinus spp.*
Pineapple	*Ananas comosus*
Pitcher plant (American)	*Sarracenia purpurea*
Pitcher plant (Asian and Australian)	*Nepenthes mixta*
Poinsettia	*Euphorbia pulcherrima*
Potato	*Solanum tuberosum*
Prickly pear	*Opuntia humifusa*
Pyrethrum	*Chrysanthemum cinerariifolium*
Rafflesia	*Rafflesia tuan-mudae*
Rata	*Metrosideros fulgens*
Red hot poker	*Kniphofia uvaria*
Red iris	*Iris fulva*
Red oak	*Quercus rubra*
Red pepper (chili)	*Capsicum frutescens*
Reed	*Phragmites communis*
Reed-mace	*Typha latifolia*
Reindeer moss	*Cetraria rangifera*
Rhododendron	*Rhododendron arboreum*
Rhubarb	*Rheum rhaponticum*
Rice	*Oryza sativa*
Rock rose	*Cistus ladaniferus*
Rosewood	*Dalbergia nigra*
Runner bean	*Phaseolus coccineus*
Rubber plant	*Ficus elastica*
Sagebrush	*Artemisia tridentata*
Sago palm	*Metroxylon sago*
Saguaro	*Carnegiea gigantea*
Sansevieria	*Sansevieria trifasciata*
Sapele	*Entandophragma cylindricum*
Saw palmetto	*Serenoa palmata*
Saxifrage	*Saxifraga oppositifolia*
Screw pine	*Pandanus odoratissimus*
Showy lady's slipper orchid	*Cypripedium reginae*
Silk-cotton tree	*Ceiba pentandra*
Skunk cabbage	*Lysichitum americanum*
Snakemouth flower	*Pogonia ophioglossoides*
Snow gum	*Eucalyptus pauciflora*
South American beech	*Nothofagus procera*
Southern catalpa	*Catalpa bignonioides*
Southern magnolia	*Magnolia grandiflora*
Sphagnum moss	*Sphagnum recurvum*
Spider plant	*Chlorophytum comosum*
Spruce	*Picea abies*
Stag's horn fern	*Platycerium hillii*
Stephanotis	*Stephanotis floribunda*
Stone plant	*Lithops gracidelineata*
Strawberry	*Fragaria chiloensis*
Strelitzia	*Strelitzia regina*
Sugar cane	*Saccharum officinarum*
Sugar maple	*Acer saccharum*
Sunflower	*Helianthus annuus*
Sungold	*Helichrysum bracteatum*
Sweet chestnut	*Castanea sativa*
Tamarisk	*Tamarix spp.*
Tea	*Camellia sinensis*
Tea-tree	*Leptospermum scoparium*
Teak	*Tectona grandis*
Thistle	*Cirsium vulgare*
Tobacco	*Nicotiana tabacum*
Toe-toe grass	*Cortaderia toetoe*
Tomato	*Lycopersicon esculentum*
Tree-daisy	*Olearia cheesmanii*
Tree fern	*Dicksonia antarctica*
Tree heath	*Erica arborea*
Trumpet-creeper	*Campsis radicans*
Tulip	*Tulipa kaufmanniana*
Vanilla orchid	*Vanilla planifolia*
Vine	*Vitis vinifera*
Vriesia	*Vriesia splendens*
Walnut	*Juglans regia*
Waratah	*Telopea speciossima*
Water melon	*Citrullus vulgaris*
Welwitschia	*Welwitschia mirabilis*
West Australian Christmas tree	*Nuytsia floribunda*
Wheat	*Triticum aestivum*
White arum lily	*Zantedeschia aethiopica*
White water lily	*Nymphaea alba*
Wild daffodil	*Narcissus pseudonarcissus*
Wild raspberry	*Rubus idaeus*
Wild rose	*Rosa pendulina*
Wild lupin	*Lupinus perennis*
Willow herb	*Epilobium angustifolium*
Woolly cactus	*Pseudoespostoa melanostela*
Yam	*Dioscorea rotundata*
Yellow buckeye	*Aesculus glabra*
Yellow water lily	*Nuphar variegatum*

Index

ebony, 52, *52–3*, 54, **56–7**, **60–1**
edelweiss, *22–3*, **24–5**, 26, **28–9**
elephant grass, **56–7**, 58, *58*, **60–1**
epiphytes, 19, 38, 80, *90–1*, 92, 102, 114
eucalypts (gum trees), 107 **108–9**, 121
Eucalyptus spp., distribution of, **123**
euphorbias, 59
Europe, 20–35; climates of, **14–15**;
    maps of, (North) **24–5**, (South) **28–9**
evening primrose, *70–1*, **72–3**, 75, **76–7**
evergreen oak, **28–9**, 80
evergreen plants, 11, 17; of
    Mediterranean climates, 16, 20

ferns, 83
fibres: baobab bark, 59; coconut, 88;
    cotton, 79; flax, 33; hemp, 50;
    jute, 43; sisal, 87
fig, *20–1*, 23, **28–9**
flame tree, 104, *104–5*, **108–9**
flamingo flower, *90–1*, 92, **94–5**
flannel flower, *107*, **108–9**, 110
flax, **24–5**, **28–9**, *31*, 32–3
flies, flowers pollinated by, 19
forests: blend of meadows and, 17, 26,
    30; *see also* coniferous, deciduous,
    temperate rain, *and* tropical rain
    forests
foxglove, **24–5**, *26*, **28–9**, 30
fringe lily, *107*, **108–9**, 110, **112–13**
fuchsia, *98–9*, 99, **103**

gentians, 18, *22–3*, 24, **24–5**, **28–9**
geraniums, **60–1**, 65, *66–7*
gladiolus, **56–7**, **60–1**, *66–7*, 67;
    distribution of, 121, **123**
glasswort, 35, **40–1**, *43*, **44–5**, 46
gourds, **56–7**, **60–1**, *62*, 63
grape vine, *20–1*, 23, **24–5**, **28–9**
grass, perennial, 30, 58; pastures of, 50,
    79, 82, 104
grassland: alpine, 18; temperate, **14–15**,
    17; tropical, **14–15**, 16
grass tree (black boy), **108–9**, *111*, 112,
    112–13
greenheart tree, 90
ground cherry (Cape gooseberry), **94–5**,
    100, *101*, **103**
growth, annual rhythm of, 10, 13, 16, 68
growth rings in trees: in temperate
    climates, 10–11, 86; in tropical
    climates, 38
guava, *92*, 93, **94–5**, **103**
Guernsey lily, 16, *16–17*
gum, kauri, 116
gum arabic (from *Acacia senegal*), **56–7**,
    60–1, *64*, 65
gum trees (eucalypts), 107, **108–9**, 121

hairs, plants covered with, 26, 98, 111
hakea, 108–9, *111*, 112
halophytes, 46
hawthorn, *8–9*, 10, *10*, **24–5**, **28–9**
hazel, **24–5**, **28–9**, *34*, 35
heather, **24–5**, **28–9**, *34*, 35
heaths, 17, 23; tree, **56–7**, **60–1**, 63, *64*
hebes, *116–17*, 117
hemlock (conifer), *70*, 71, **72–3**, 74,
    76–7
hemlock (plant), **28–9**, *32*, 35
hemp, **40–1**, **44–5**, 50, *50*
hibiscus, *38–9*, **40–1**, 42, **44–5**
Himalayas, 49–50
holly, 11, **28–9**
honey locust tree, *74–5*, **76–7**, 79, **84–5**
hop, **24–5**, **28–9**, *31*, 33
Hottentot fig, 67
hyacinth, **40–1**, *42*, 46

ice-caps, **14–15**, 17, *17*
insectivorous plants, 86, *113*, 114, 116
insects, flowers pollinated by, 10, *12*, 13,
    24, 55, 75; *see also* bees, flies, moths,
    wasps
ipomoea (morning glory), 92, **94–5**
iris: red (N. America), *75*, **76–7**, 79–80,
    84–5; yellow flag (Europe), **24–5**, *32*,
    35
ivy, *8–9*, *10*, 11, **24–5**, **28–9**

jacaranda tree, *92*, **94–5**, 96, **103**
jack pine, 70
Japan, 49
Joshua tree, **76–7**, *82*, **84–5**, 87
Judas tree, 23
juniper, 17; in Asia, **40–1**, **44–5**, 50;
    in Europe, 23, **24–5**, **28–9**;
    in N. America, *68–9*, **70–1**, *72–3*,
    76–7
jute, *38*, **40–1**, 43

kangaroo paw flower, **108–9**, *111*, 112
kapok, 90
karri gum tree, **108–9**, 111, *111*
kauri pine, **108–9**, **115**, 116
kohlrabi, 33
kokkerboom tree, *66*
koromiko, **115**, *116–17*, 117
kowhai, **115**, *116–17*, 117

lantern hakea, *see* hakea
larch, *22–3*, **24–5**, 26, **28–9**, 50
leaf bases, estimation of age of plant
    from counts of, 112, 114
leaves, 10; photosynthesis in, 11–12
legumes, 32, 63, 97
lentil, 32
lianas, 80
lichens, *16–17*, 17, 35, 71
linen, 32
linseed, 33
longleaf pine, *78*, 80
lotus, 36, *36–7*, 38, **40–1**
lupin, wild blue, **72–3**, **76–7**, *80*, 86

mace, 42
madrone, **72–3**, **76–7**, *83*, **84–5**, 88
magnolia, southern, **76–7**, *78*, 80, **84–5**
mahogany tree, **76–7**, **84–5**, *86–7*, 88,
    90, **94–5**
maidenhair tree (*Ginkgo*), **40–1**, **44–5**,
    46–7, 49
maize, 62, **94–5**, 100, *101*, **103**;
    distribution of, 118, 120, **122**
mango, *38*, **40–1**, 42
maple, *68–9*, **72–3**, **76–7**; sugar, 68
maquis, 23
meadow, blend of forest and, 17, 26, 30
Mediterranean climate, **14–15**, 16, 20,
    104, 112
mescal (button cactus), **76–7**, *83*, **84–5**,
    87
mesembryanthemum, **60–1**, *66–7*, 67
mesquite, **76–7**, *83*, **84–5**, 88
mid-latitude climates, **14–15**, 17
millets, **56–7**, **60–1**, 62–3, *63*
mineral salts, required by plants, 11, *12*
mistletoe, *8–9*, 11, *11*, **24–5**, **28–9**
monkey-puzzle tree (Chile pine), 99, *99*,
    103
monkshood, *12*, 13
Monterey pine, distribution of, 121, **123**
Moreton Bay chestnut, *107*, **108–9**, 110
mosses, *16–17*, 17, 35, 83
moths, flowers pollinated by, 75
mountain climates, 13, **14–15**, 18, 20,
    26, 63, 106, 116
mulberry, **40–1**, **44–5**, *46–7*, 49
mushroom, **24–5**, **28–9**, *30–1*, 33

nasturtium, **94–5**, 98, *98–9*, **103**
nectaries of flowers, *13*
New England, 71
New Guinea, 112, 114, 116; map of,
    112–13
New Zealand, 114, *116–17*; map of, **115**
nitrogen, required by plants, 11; fixed by
    legumes from the air, 32, 64, 86, 97
noon flower, **108–9**, *110*, 111

temperate rain forest, 82
temperature, and growth, 8, *12*, 13, *13*, 16
thatchpalm, Jamaica, **76–7**, *78*, 80, **84–5**
thistle, **24–5**, **28–9**, *30–1*, 33
tobacco, **94–5**, 100, *100*, **103**; distribution of, 120, **123**
toe-toe (tussock) grass, *114*, **115**, 117
tomato, **94–5**, 100, *100*, **103**; distribution of, 121, **122**
transpiration, 13, 16
tree-daisy (*Olearia*), **115**, *116–17*, 117
tree ferns, **108–9**, **112–13**, *114*, **115**, 116
trees: conifers, 26; deciduous, 10, 26
tropical climates, **14–15**, 16, 112
tropical grassland, **14–15**, 16, 58–9, 62–5
tropical highland, **14–15**, 16
tropical rain forest, **14–15**, 16, *17*, 18, 19; in Africa, 52, *52–3*; in S. America, 90, *90–1*; in Australasia, 107, 114
trumpet-creeper, **76–7**, *79*, 80, **84–5**
tubers, 55, 88, 96, 100
tulip, **40–1**, *42*, **44–5**, 46
tundra, **14–15**, 17, 25, 35, 50, 68, 71
Turkey, *42*

vanilla orchid, *92–3*, **94–5**, 98
vriesia, 104, *104–5*, **108–9**

walnut, **40–1**, *42*, **44–5**, 46
waratah, 104, *104–5*, **108–9**
wasps, pollination by, 23
water: absorbed by roots, 11; lost in transpiration, 13; needed for growth, 13, 16; plants adapted to life in, 10; seeds carried by, 10, *87*, 88
water lilies: blue (Australia), **108–9**, *110–11*, 111, **112–13**; giant Amazon,

90–1, 92, **94–5**; white (Europe), *8–9*, 11, **24–5**, **28–9**; yellow (N. America), *68–9*, 70, **72–3**, **76–7**
water melon, *54*, 55, **56–7**, 58, **60–1**
wattle, golden, 104, *104–5*, 106, **108–9**
wax, leaves coated with, 11, 16, 46, 64, 87, 101
Welwitschia mirabilis, **60–1**, *66–7*, 67
wheat, *8–9*, **24–5**, **28–9**, **40–1**, *42*, 46, 62, 82; distribution of, 118, 120, **122**
Wickham, Sir Henry, 96, 121
willow, 24, 50; dwarf, **44–5**, *50*, 50–1
willow herb, rosebay (fireweed), **24–5**, *26*, **28–9**, 31
wind: flowers pollinated by, 8, 10, 67; seeds carried by, 10, 13, 19, 31, 35
woolly cactus, **94–5**, *99*, **103**

yam (*Dioscorea*), 55, *55*, **56–7**, **60–1**,
yuccas, 16

Acknowledgment:

Page 31 spear thistle after Lorus and Margery Milne, *Living Plants of the World,* Chanticleer Press, Inc., New York, and Thomas Nelson & Sons Ltd., London, 1967.
(Photo Bill Ratcliffe)

D. L.: M-15.152 - 1973.